Roland Schrapp

The Mirroring of Life before Birth in the Seven-Year Periods of Human Life on Earth

CW01334936

Roland Schrapp

The Mirroring of Life before Birth in the Seven-Year Periods of Human Life on Earth

The Deutsche Nationalbibliothek (German National Library) lists this publication in the Deutsche Nationalbibliografie (German National Bibliography).
Detailed bibliographic data are available on the Internet at www.dnb.de.

© 2023 Roland Schrapp

Production and Publishing: BoD – Books on Demand, Norderstedt (Germany)

ISBN: 9783743124585

"Between death and rebirth we expand beyond the starry sky, and we bring its powers into life and feel them as the most significant powers of our soul. No wonder, since we are the outward image of it!"

Rudolf Steiner, GA 140, lecture of February 17, 1913

"From a spiritual-scientific point of view, man does not only originate from the sense world, but from the spiritual foundations of the world, which stand behind the outer sense perceptible world; so that man is born out of the sense world only as a sense perceptible being. But in so far as the sense perceptible human body is permeated by spirit and soul, man is born as spirit and soul out of the spirit and soul of the cosmos."

Rudolf Steiner, GA 58, lecture of December 9, 1909

English edition of the German book "Spiegelungen des vorgeburtlichen Daseins des Menschen in den Jahrsiebten des Erdenlebens".

Contents

Man, a Cosmic Being

The Four Kingdoms of Nature and the Fourfold Structure of the Human Being

Generally, the human being is considered the culmination of the biological evolution on the earth. However, natural science does not concede mankind to be an independent fourth kingdom of nature, besides the three kingdoms of minerals, plants, and animals. Instead, it places man, with reference to Darwinism, only at the upper end of the animal series and assigns him as the genus "Homo" (man) to the family of the "Hominidae" (great apes), together with the three other genera "Gorilla", "Pongo" (orangutan) and "Pan" (chimpanzee and bonobo). In this way the human being is degraded to a highly developed animal, despite the fact that he ascended during the course of the evolutionary development to the level of "Homo sapiens", the "wise" or "understanding" human being.

This conclusion by the natural science is seemingly confirmed by numerous similarities of humans with the above-mentioned three genera of great apes. However, it is obvious that such an assessment is based on a rather superficial approach, since besides the obvious similarities there are nevertheless quite serious differences.

First, there is the ability of rational thinking, which only humans have. Furthermore, they can communicate their trains of thought, feelings and intentions to others through language. A third, purely human characteristic is the upright stance and walk, which even the highest species of monkeys can only perform for a short time.

These three striking features can be directly observed in every human being, provided that there is no disease or handicap that would hinder them. In addition, there is a fourth highly significant characteristic. This is the consciousness of oneself. It enables the human being to experience her/himself as an independent "I", to call oneself also by the word "I" and furthermore to develop a fully conscious, intellectual and creative activity. That is why humans are called "Homo sapiens" even by natural science.

If one compares the immediate environment, in which the three above-mentioned great ape species live, with the environment, in which humans live, then a considerable, even downright gigantic difference shows up. Great apes change the natural conditions, which they find in their environment, only in small measure, at most to prepare a nest to sleep in. In this they resemble the other beings of the animal kingdom. Nest-building is a behaviour that runs through the entire animal kingdom as a characteristic common to many animal species.

Humans, however, design their environment completely new! Out of fully conscious creative, intellectual productivity, they plan and build houses, roads, bridges, devices, vehicles, including those which can fly and even reach the outer space. In addition, they make clothing to protect their bodies. No other species on earth creates its own environment and protection to such a degree and so comprehensively. Unfortunately, this is still often done in a way that is harmful to nature and the environment. Fortunately, however, a change in thinking is now taking place.

In view of these exorbitant differences between human beings and animals, who could doubt that mankind forms a completely independent, fourth kingdom of the earth, which considerably surpasses the animal kingdom.

As far as the ability of the language is concerned, this is already present in a rudimentary form in most of the highly developed animal species. But there it serves only for the expression of emotional states, such as pleasure and suffering, as well as for voicing attracting or warning calls. Animals share their emotions, the state of their soul, with their fellow species. They do not discuss scientific questions such as whether the sun revolves around the earth or vice versa. They do not develop philosophical or religious views, do not ask whether the world was created by God or came into being in a miraculous way by a Big Bang. The interest of humans, on the other hand, is not limited to the earth and the present, but extends far out into the cosmos, asking even about its origin and goal.

If we look at the four kingdoms of nature with regard to their main characteristics, one can say that the fundamental property of the mineral kingdom is *materiality*. Indeed, we find material components also in the bodies of plants, animals and people. However, these bodies are animated. In them, *life* is moreover expressed as a higher, independent principle. Unlike the plants, animals have emotions which they express in a rich and varied soul life. They are endowed with an indwelling *soul*. In addition to the above, humans alone are endowed with an indwelling *spirit*.

Figure 1 shows the connection between the four kingdoms of nature and the four modes of existence, substance, life, soul and spirit.

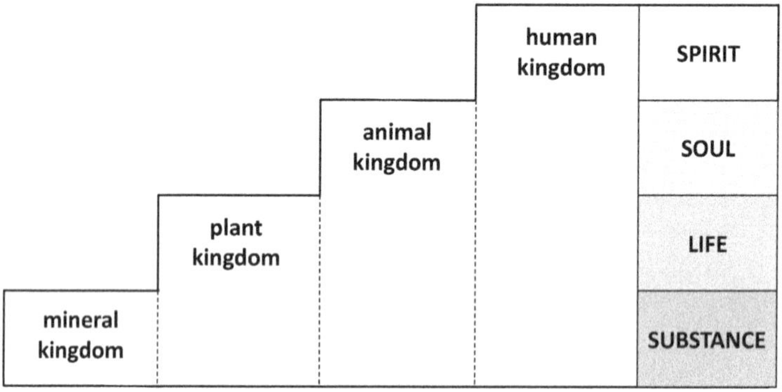

Figure 1: The four kingdoms of the earth and the four modes of existence

The presence of these four principles in man is unmistakably expressed in the structure of the human body. The head is the organ where the spirit expresses its self-consciousness and individuality, known as the Self or the "I". This "I" is of a spiritual nature and is the highest member of the human being. The human countenance is an expression of this individuality. Hence, to identify a person by means of an identity card, only a photo of the face is required rather than of the whole body.

Unlike the spirit, which we connect to our head, we feel our soul and our emotional life connected to our chest area, especially to our heart. Here, with the help of our lungs, the rhythmic breathing takes place, which we have in common with all soul-endowed beings, including the animals. The corresponding member, which serves as a carrier of the soul, is called soul body or astral body.

Lower still, in the abdominal cavity, the nutrients supplied from outside are processed to nourish and keep the body alive. A comparable activity also takes place in the plant and animal kingdoms. The carrier of these vital functions is the life or etheric body.

With the four limbs attached to the trunk, the human being enters into direct contact with the outer physical world. To that effect, we possess a suitably formed physical body; with our legs and feet we move about, with arms and hands we perform our deeds and feed ourselves with earthly nourishment.

The human form is obviously based on a fourfold structure. which proves that humans, as the fourth kingdom of nature, unite and surpass the three lower kingdoms, namely, animal, plant and mineral kingdom.

SPIRIT	"I"	head
SOUL	astral body	chest
LIFE	etheric body	abdomen
SUBSTANCE	physical body	limbs

Figure 2: The four members of the human being in relation to the human form

A further examination reveals that the human being can be organized in other ways, as the following chapters will show.

The Threefold Structure of the Human Being according to the Divine Trinity

In antiquity, the prevailing view was that it is above all the spirit which makes the human being a human being. The spirit distinguishes the human being in a special way and raises mankind above the animal kingdom, which is only endowed with a soul. This is inherent in the German word "Mensch" as well as in the English word "man". They are late forms of the Latin term "mens" and the related Sanskrit term "manas", which both mean "spirit, ability to think, mind".

Both the pre-Christian religions and Christianity itself regard the world and man as created by a supreme deity who reveals himself outwardly as threefold. In Christianity, the triune and at the same time threefold Godhead is called Father, Son and Holy Spirit. But already in the older religions we find a supreme trinity, as for example the Trimurti of Hinduism, consisting of Brahma, Vishnu and Shiva. According to the original teachings of mankind, the human being was created in the image of the Godhead: threefold, consisting of body, soul and spirit.

So long as people had an innate clairvoyance, this knowledge of the trichotomy, the threefold structure of the human being, was a matter of course to them. But the increasing turning of their attention to the physical, earthly outside world caused a gradual waning of the original clairvoyant ability. Soon they lost not only the extrasensory perception, but also the understanding for the spirit as the highest member of the human being.

Thus, even before the end of the first Christian millennium, the bishops at the Council of Constantinople in 869 made the dogmatic decision that man only consists of body and soul, the latter having at most some spiritual qualities. The spirit as an independent part of the human being was denied and trichotomy, the threefold structure of the human being, was condemned as heresy.

Before the end of the second millennium, even the understanding of the soul as an independent component of the human being was finally lost and the scientific view prevailed that man consists only of a body, which in an as yet inexplicable way, expresses the epiphenomenon of a soul life, which, consequently, ceases with the death of the physical body.

Thus the conception for the existence of the human being as soul and spirit after the death no longer had any basis. The widespread materialism of today has no understanding for the independent existence of the soul and spirit.

The originally vertical world view of mankind, which still stretched far beyond the sense world into the suprasensory regions of the soul and spirit worlds, gradually gave way to a horizontal view, limited to the physical sense perceptible world. With this came the illusion that one can explain the world as well as the human being solely from matter and its ever further fragmentation into atoms and elementary particles. Compared with the older, far more comprehensive world views one can certainly say that today's fixation on matter has practically reduced human striving for knowledge to a crawling in the dust.

The primal knowledge of mankind, on the other hand, still comprised three planes of existence or worlds to which the human being belongs and over which he extends as a spiritual, soul and physical being. In each of these three worlds also the two other worlds find their expression, so that each world proves itself again as threefold.

The physical world can thus be divided into:

- the fixed stars, as an expression of the basic characteristic of the spiritual world: the realm of duration or eternity,
- the planetary world with the rhythmic course of sun, moon and planets as expression of the basic characteristic of the soul world: the flowing time,
- and the terrestrial world, the basic characteristic of which is static space.

This macrocosmic threefold structure can also be understood in the physical body of the earthly human being:

- The head as the uppermost part of the body and seat of the spirit imitates the vault of heaven in its spherical shape, in the round curvature of the skull.
- The chest, the seat of the soul, with its rhythmic breathing activity and heartbeat, reveals an inner connection with the rhythms of the planetary movement.
- The abdomen and the limbs show their direct relationship to the physical materiality of the earthly outside world.

Thus, to earlier cultures, the earthly human being was regarded as a microcosm, formed after the great archetype, the macrocosm. Man was therefore understood as a cosmic spirit- and soul-being, which periodically descends into the earthly body, in order to gather experiences that can only be obtained through a bodily existence at a particular age.

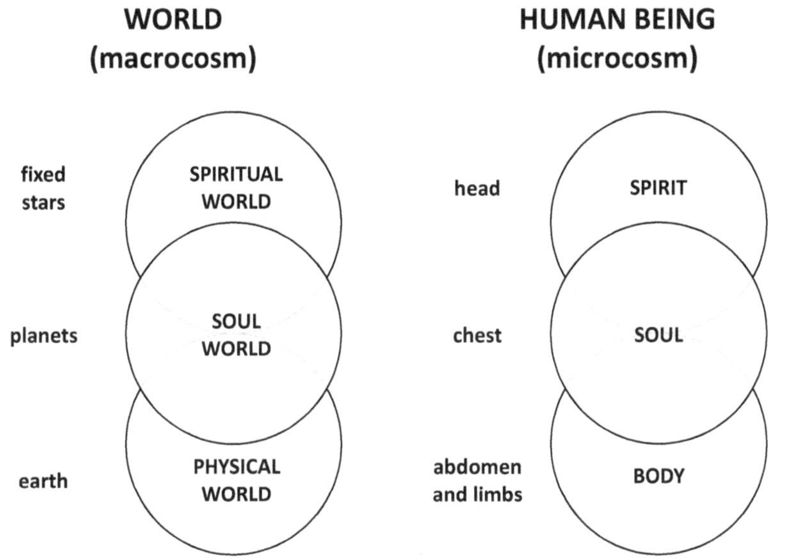

Figure 3:
The human being as a microcosmic image of the macrocosm

The Sevenfold Structure of the Human Being according to the Planetary Spheres

Not only the entire human body, but also its parts indicate their relationship with the cosmos. For example, if we look at the life processes alone, we see that they have a sevenfold structure, according to the seven "traditional" planets known to man in ancient times.

As already mentioned, the rhythmic course of the planets is the physical expression of the soul world. However, as Figure 3 shows, this projects down into the upper half of the physical world. Thereby, the characteristic of rhythm is imprinted on the substance and thus brings about the rhythmical life processes.

Rudolf Steiner represented the connection of the seven life activities with the seven planets in the following diagram:[1]

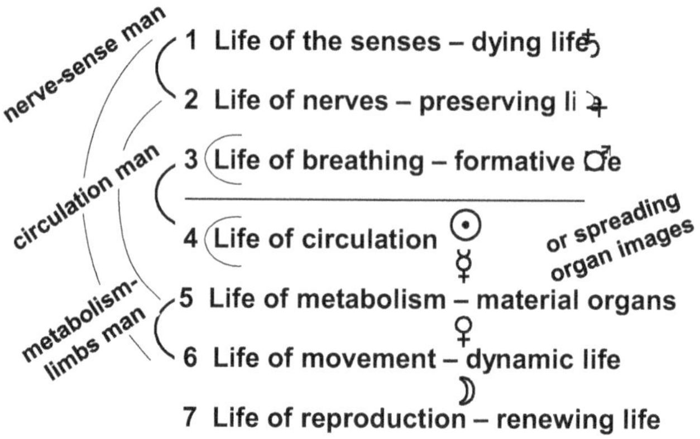

Figure 4: The seven life activities of the earthly human body

This list shows in which way the sevenfold structure finds its expression. The *spiritual* part of the human being expresses itself on the level of life activities in two parts, as life of the senses (1) and life of the nerves (2). Rudolf Steiner summarized both activities with the term "the nerve-sense man". The *soul* part of man finds its twofold expression in the life of breathing (3) and the life of circulation (4), which Rudolf Steiner summarized as "circulation man".

---

1 GA 208 "Anthroposophie als Kosmosophie – Teil II" (Anthroposophy as Cosmosophy – Part II), Dornach, lecture of October 29, 1921.

Finally, the life of metabolism (5) and the life of movement (6) constitute the actual b o d i l y part, the "metabolism-limbs man".

Basically, the human being is completely described with these six life activities. The life of reproduction (7), in addition gives the possibility to create a completely new, again six- or sevenfold human being.

In his diagram, Rudolf Steiner obviously used the planetary signs of Mercury and Venus in the Copernican sense, according to which Mercury is the closest and Venus the second closest planet to the sun. This is also evident from the corresponding lecture, in which Rudolf Steiner referred to the physical orbital periods of the planets, as well as to the fact that the outer planets Saturn, Jupiter and Mars are temporarily "obscured" by the sun during their orbit, whereas the inner planets Mercury and Venus temporarily "obscure" the sun.

From the occult point of view, the planet Mercury, passing in front of the Sun, as seen from Earth, marks the outer limit of the Venus sphere. And the planet Venus, passing in front of the Sun, marks the outer limit of the Mercury sphere. Mercury, the god of travellers, was regarded in ancient times as the regent of man's movement life, which is expressed primarily in the lower limbs as the physical means of locomotion. They originate in the hip region and thus above the region of the reproductive organs. On the other hand, the main metabolic organs, which prepare food substances for absorption into the bloodstream, are located in the upper abdomen, just below the diaphragm. Metabolism, from an ancient and occult point of view, is ruled by Venus. In addition to being the goddess of love and beauty, Venus also rules fructification of gardens and of nature. Therefore, the occult order of the planetary spheres is not Moon, Venus, Mercury, Sun, but Moon, Mercury, Venus, Sun, and so on.

The Twelvefold Structure of the Human Being according to the Zodiac

Figure 5:
The twelvefold division of the human being according to the zodiac (from the Book of Hours of the Duke of Berry)

If one considers the earthly human body not according to its vital functions, but according to its outer form, then instead of a sevenfold structure according to the planets, a twelvefold structure according to the zodiac results. This shows that man in reality originates from the region of the fixed stars, the part of the world through which the spiritual world expresses itself (cf. Figure 3, page 17). As cosmic spiritual beings, we also receive in our earthly life an outer form which follows exactly the sequence of the zodiacal forces from the crown of the head to the feet, beginning at the top with Aries and ending at the bottom with Pisces. Probably the best-known representation of this primal knowledge of mankind that survived into the Middle Ages, is shown in the adjacent illustration, which dates from the 15th century.

In reality, the human being is not at all an earthling that we usually think of.

Earlier cultures, far less firmly bound to the physical sense perception and the material as it is the case today, knew not only about the structure of the human being according to cosmic principles, namely the seven-foldness of the life functions and the twelve-foldness of its form, they moreover possessed clear knowledge, that man is a spirit- and soul-being, which is at home in the cosmos. They knew, that humans enter into an earthly body for a few decades after having spent several centuries in the hereafter, in order to gather experiences, which can only be gained on earth and which are evaluated and subsequently transformed into new abilities in the existence between two earthly lives, in the course of a purely cosmic existence.

This wisdom was increasingly lost to mankind during the last millennia, especially to the western world. Instead, humanity was assigned the task of directing attention more and more to the outer material world, the physical nature, in order to develop a logically structured, scientific thinking, as well as an I-consciousness, which clearly distinguishes itself from the outside world. This turning to the physical inevitably led the western part of humanity - Central and Western Europe as well as the countries further west - towards the theoretical materialism, which attempts to explain the world and man only on the basis of the material.

But by the middle of the 18th century, both the ability to think scientifically and the realization of the great importance of the human "I" had matured to such an extent that in Central Europe the foremost philosophers could begin to use the newly acquired tool of scientific thinking to penetrate into higher levels of existence from an expanded perspective and with fully conscious thought processes. They strove to supplement the science of nature with a science of the soul and spirit, for they believed that only in this way could one arrive at a comprehensive understanding of man and the world.

Without a doubt, the "German idealism" played a leading role here. In the 19th century, it produced one of its most significant blossoms with the philosophical triumvirate of J. G. Fichte, Fr. W. J. Schelling and G. W. Fr. Hegel.[2] Unlike their predecessor Immanuel Kant[3], who with his "critical idealism" still set strict limits to human knowledge based on restricted logic, they came to the insight that the human soul with the "I" was quite capable of penetrating to that spirit which underlies both nature and man in creative activity.[4] In this way they laid an extremely important preliminary foundation for a science of the spirit. It thus became later possible for Rudolf Steiner to found Anthroposophy in Germany, as he himself said:

"For the German people is called to transform its idealism into living spiritual knowledge. Fichte, Schelling, Hegel, who are so attacked today, have created a thinking which is not yet spiritualism, not yet spiritual science, but is the germ for spiritual science, which, so to speak, if it is meditated, really leads to spiritual science."[5]

Further important spirited contributions, which prepared the ground for Rudolf Steiner's anthroposophy, were made by the theologian and philosopher Immanuel Hermann Fichte (1796 - 1879), the son of J. G. Fichte, with his "Anthropology". In addition, vital contributions were made by the poet, naturalist and philosopher

---

[2] Johann Gottlieb Fichte (1762 – 1814), Friedrich Wilhelm Joseph Schelling (1775 – 1854) und Georg Wilhelm Friedrich Hegel (1770 – 1831)

[3] Immanuel Kant (1724 – 1804), philosopher from the former German city of Königsberg (today Kaliningrad, Russia).

[4] See, for example, Rudolf Steiner's books GA 20 "Vom Menschenrätsel" (On the Riddle of Man) and GA 18 "Rätsel der Philosophie" (Riddles of Philosophy).

[5] GA 159 "Das Geheimnis des Todes – Wesen und Bedeutung Mitteleuropas und die europäischen Volksgeister" (Mystery of Death – Nature and Significance of Central Europe and the European Folk Spirits), Nuremberg, lecture of March 14, 1915.

Johann Wolfgang von Goethe (1749 - 1832) with his theory of metamorphosis, as well as by the poet and philosopher Gotthold Ephraim Lessing (1729 - 1781) with his "aesthetic writings". On the basis of an independent inner contemplation, all three thinkers arrived at the realization of reincarnation of the human immortal spirit- and soul-being.

I. H. Fichte said the following about the deceased soul: *"To its organizational power only has to be presented another means of embodiment in order to appear in new bodily activity."* [6]

Goethe wrote in a letter to Johann Daniel Falk[7]: *"I am sure that as you see me here, I have been there a thousand times and I hope to return a thousand times."*

Lessing expressed his conviction by asking, *"Why should I not return as often as I am adept in acquiring new knowledge, new skills?"* and *"Is this idea so ridiculous, then, because it is the oldest?"* [8]

These Central European thinkers came to the knowledge of reincarnation by their own spiritual power, not by taking over Indian teachings. These were made known to the West only in 1875 by H. P. Blavatsky. [9]

---

6 I. H. Fichte: "Anthropologie" (Anthropology), §§ 133 und 134

7 Johann Daniel Falk (1768 – 1826), writer and poet of evangelical hymns

8 From Lessing's 1780 work "Die Erziehung des Menschengeschlechts" (The Education of the Human Race).

9 Helena Petrovna Blavatsky (1831 - 1891), born in Ekaterinoslav (now Dnipro, Ukraine) to Peter von Hahn, an officer from Mecklenburg (Germany), and Yelena von Hahn (née Fadeyeva), a Russian writer. H. P. Blavatsky, spiritualist medium and author of esoteric books, founded the Theosophical Society together with Henry Steel Olcott in New York City in 1875, through which excerpts from the traditional Indian spiritual teachings became known to a wider public in the Western world.

At the beginning of the 20th century, Rudolf Steiner (1861 – 1925) expressed himself from his own spiritual research in the same sense:

"Why should our soul actually enter again and again into an earthly body, if it didn't just have something new to experience every time, but also something new to sense and feel? By the fact that also the abilities of the people and the intimacies of soul life are always new and changing, it is possible for our soul not only to climb from step to step as if on a staircase, but each time there is also an opportunity for it to take in something new from outside, because of the changing life conditions of our earth. It is not merely through its transgressions, through its karmic sins, that our soul is led from incarnation to incarnation; but because our earth changes in all its conditions of life, it is possible for our soul to take in new things again and again also from outside." [10]

However, the transformation of the gained experiences into new abilities takes place only in the existence between two incarnations in the higher worlds, which have their physical expression in the extra-terrestrial cosmos. There the human being stays for several centuries. Hence Rudolf Steiner made the significant statement:

"In reality, the human being is not an earthly being. In reality the human being is a cosmic being, a being belonging to the whole universe." [11]

That is the very reason why the earthly human body has a threefold, sevenfold and twelvefold structure corresponding to the macrocosm.

---

10 GA 116 "Der Christus-Impuls und die Entwicklung des Ich-Bewusstseins" (The Christ Impulse and the Development of I-Consciousness), Berlin, lecture of October 25, 1909.

11 GA 200 "Die neue Geistigkeit und das Christuserlebnis des 20. Jahrhunderts" (The New Spirituality and the Experience of Christ in the 20th Century), Dornach, lecture of October 31, 1920.

Divisions of the Course of Life on Earth

Now that it has been established that both the life functions and the physical form of man are structured according to the numbers three, seven and twelve, should we not be allowed to assume that man's earthly course of life also shows a division according to the same cosmic principles?

In the first third of life on earth, bodily development predominates. Within the period of 3 x 7 years the small, recumbent figure of a new-born child develops to an upright standing and walking adult. An equal division in the middle of life is less visible outwardly, because it takes place mainly in the inner life of the soul. Finally, in the last, third phase of life on earth, spiritual interests come to the fore in those who have preserved their capacity for development into old age. And since the spirit is the opposite pole of the body, the onset of the people's spiritualization, which is to lead them back to their heavenly home, is marked by degeneration of the material corporeality. In this sense, man's earthly course of life is also divided into sections according to the threefold structure of body, soul and spirit in accord with the divine Trinity.

If one looks at the human life on earth from the planetary perspective, it proves to be sevenfold in a similar way as it is the case with the life functions. Rudolf Steiner explained in one of his lectures that with the help of the two higher levels of consciousness "Imagination" and "Inspiration", by way of the ether body, the bearer of the life functions , an insight into the experiences of man after death is possible, in those regions of the soul world and the lower spiritual world, which have their physical expression in the seven traditional planets. If at a certain age, a person looks back at the stages of life he has already passed, he will find them connected with certain planetary spheres. From the age of 63 on, it becomes possible to have access to all seven planetary spheres. [12]

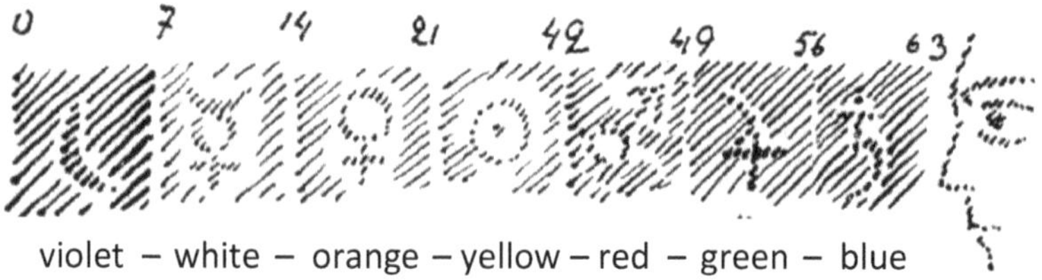

Figure 6: Rudolf Steiner's sketch on the connection of the course of human life with the seven planetary spheres

As the above sketch shows, there is a peculiarity concerning the Sun sphere. Rudolf Steiner assigned to it three seven-year periods: the 4th to 6th, which correspond to the period from 21 to 42 years.

In other lectures Rudolf Steiner described the connection of the human course of life with the evolution of our planetary system. He also elaborated on the influence of the spiritual beings on the seven-year periods of human life on earth, with whom humans cooperate between the two incarnations. A detailed presentation of these perspectives, which also affect the course of human life is beyond the scope of this book. The interested reader is referred to the corresponding lectures by Rudolf Steiner.[13]

---

12 GA 236 "Esoterische Betrachtungen karmischer Zusammenhänge - Band II", (Karmic Relationships – Vol. 2) Dornach, lecture of May 29, 1924.

13 GA 96 "Ursprungsimpulse der Geisteswissenschaft" (Original Impulses of Spiritual Science), Berlin, lecture of March 4, 1907, as well as GA 236 "Esoterische Betrachtungen karmischer Zusammenhänge - Band II" (Karmic Relationships - Vol. 2), Dornach, lecture of May 18, 1924.

A completely different type of division results if one considers the entire human incarnation cycle between two incarnations, which extends over the twelve planes of existence. They, too, are mirrored in the seven-year periods of the earthly course of life and, accordingly, contribute to a twelvefold perspective on earthly life.

When we use the term "humanity", we usually mean only the people living on earth in a physical body. However, they constitute only a small part of the total humanity. Even in our times, when we speak of "overpopulation", a much larger number of people occupy higher realms of existence, where experiences of their past earthly lives are transformed into new and higher abilities for future earthly lives. This process takes place in cooperation with the spiritual beings of the higher worlds. It is during this cooperation that the spiritual archetype of the future earthly human body is created. Rudolf Steiner pointed out this important fact several times, namely,

"that only during his time on earth man is confined to a certain place, only during his time on earth he occupies a small space, while during the whole time between death and rebirth he is incorporated into the planetary system and, still later after death, even into the world beyond. If we often say about the development between birth and death, to express an occult fact, that man shows himself as a kind of microcosmic image of the macrocosm, we must now say: Between death and rebirth, man himself is actually macrocosmic; he is poured into the macrocosm; he proves himself then quite a macrocosmic being, for in this interim he must draw from the macrocosm the forces he needs for his next incarnation." [14]

[14] GA 140 "Okkulte Untersuchungen über das Leben zwischen Tod und neuer Geburt" (Occult Investigations into the Life between Death and New Birth), Munich, lecture of November 28, 1912.

During this macrocosmic phase of our existence, we work out our destiny of the next earth life with the support of higher spiritual beings. This enables us to balance out the accumulated negative karma, i.e. debts of fate, which we have caused by faulty thinking, feeling and acting. In this way, we advance in our development stage by stage and pave the way to higher levels of existence at the end of earth's evolution.

Figure 7 shows the twelve planes of existence within which the cosmic development of today's humanity takes place. The lowest plane corresponds to the existence in the physical world, the earth life. Above it are seven planetary planes of existence, which extend over the soul world and the lower spiritual world, as well as four stellar planes of existence in the higher spiritual world, which are connected with the fixed stars. [15]

In a similar way as the earthly human walks on the earth and touches it only with the soles of his feet, while the head points out into the cosmos, the entire human earth life corresponds, so to speak, solely to the "feet" of the cosmic man, while his "head" reaches up to the uppermost boundary of the spiritual world. The earthly human form is thus a symbol of the entire macrocosmic human being, completely in the sense of Goethe's saying: "Everything transient is only a likeness."

---

[15] See e.g. GA 9 "Theosophie" (Theosophy), chapter "Die drei Welten" (The three worlds) as well as GA 141 "Das Leben zwischen dem Tod und einer neuen Geburt im Verhältnis zu den kosmischen Tatsachen" (Life between Death and Rebirth in Relation to the Cosmic Facts), Berlin, lecture of April 1, 1913.

The 12 planes of existence, within which today's humanity is evolving					The 14 stages of experience of the human incarnation cycle
			2nd region	Budhi-plane	14
			1st region		13
4 stellar planes of existence	background of the fixed star sky	12	7th region	higher spiritual world	12
		11	6th region		11
		10	5th region		10
	sphere of the zodiac	9	4th region		9
7 planetary planes of existence	Saturn sphere	8	3rd region	lower spiritual world	8
	Jupiter sphere	7	2nd region		7
	Mars sphere	6	1st region		6
	Sun sphere	5	7th region	higher soul world	5
	Venus sphere	4	6th region		4
	Mercury sphere	3	5th region		3
			4th region		
	Moon sphere	2	1st – 3rd region	lower soul world	2
physical world	Earth	1			1

Figure 7:
The 12 planes of existence and
the 14 stages of experience of the human being

Regarding the individual spheres, the soul world has two peculiarities. On the one hand the Moon sphere consists of three regions of the soul world, while otherwise each region corresponds to a single planetary sphere. Secondly, the 4th region of the soul world, which is also called the "region of pleasure and displeasure", lies b e t w e e n the Moon sphere and the Mercury sphere, as a transition from the lower to the higher soul world. Rudolf Steiner explains:

"Up to the region of pleasure and displeasure, that is, up to where the soul is, as it were, between the moon and Mercury, it is still intimately afflicted with longing for its last life on earth." [16]

The spiritual world is sometimes also referred to as the "world of reason" or by the Indian term "Devachan", which means "dwelling of the gods". Accordingly, instead of lower and higher spiritual world one speaks then of the lower and upper Devachan. Above this is the so-called Budhi[17] plane, known as the "world of the providence" in western terminology. A sojourn there is possible only for human beings who have already reached extraordinarily high levels of development and are active in the service of Christ for the benefit of mankind. In Eastern terms they are called Bodhisattvas and Buddhas.

"Thus, between two incarnations, the Bodhisattva beings ascend to the Budhi plane, and up to the Budhi plane reaches that which fully consciously meets them as a teacher: the being of Christ. On the Budhi plane the Bodhisattvas and the Christ meet." There, like twelve disciples, they are grouped around Christ as the thirteenth in their midst and receive from him as teachings *"that which they have to carry down to earth".* [18]

According to Rudolf Steiner, in the middle between two incarnations even less highly developed people may be allowed a

---

16 GA 141 "Das Leben zwischen dem Tod und einer neuen Geburt im Verhältnis zu den kosmischen Tatsachen" (Life between Death and Rebirth in Relation to the Cosmic Facts), Berlin, lecture of April 1, 1913.

17 The term "Budhi" is related to "Bodhi". Hence, beings living on the Budhi plane are called "Bodhisattvas". The term "Buddha" is a participle, meaning "awaken". In Rudolf Steiner's lectures we find both the spelling "Budhi" and "Buddhi".

18 GA 116 "Der Christus-Impuls und die Entwicklung des Ich-Bewusstseins" (The Christ Impulse and the Development of I-Consciousness), Berlin, lecture of October 25, 1909, towards the end of the lecture.

glimpse into the lower regions of the sublime Budhi plane with the beings active in it:

"As I was saying, between death and rebirth man ascends to the upper Devachan or the World of Reason. There he looks into higher worlds, worlds he cannot himself enter, and there he sees those Higher Beings at work. While man spends his life in worlds extending between the physical plane and the Devachan plane, it is normal for a Bodhisattva-being to ascend to the Budhi plane, which in Europe we call the World of Providence. This is a good word, because it is their task to guide the world from age to age with providence." [19]

With which level of consciousness a human being experiences his passage through the higher worlds depends decisively on his stage of development. An individual, who adopts during earthly life only the common materialistic world view and rejects the existence of higher worlds, will after death bring only a few points of reference from his earthly life, which can serve as a basis for a fully conscious development in the higher worlds. Much will then be lived through in dreams, sometimes even in deep sleep. In such a case, the person will incarnate again on earth relatively soon, unlike those people who ascend to the higher worlds with a rich spiritually endowed consciousness. The latter have internalized much that can be further developed and transformed into new abilities in communion with higher spiritual beings.

In total, we pass through fourteen rather than through twelve stages of experience during our incarnation cycles, as shown in the right half of Figure 7 (page 29). Without any experiences that reach beyond the twelve planes of existence, we would remain enclosed in the "three worlds" and we would be denied the possibility of evolving in the direction of the Budhi plane.

---

[19] Ibidem.

It is noteworthy that Rudolf Steiner based his "Soul Calendar" on fourteen stages of experience. However, he condensed the experiences of the spheres of Jupiter and Saturn, so that thirteen verses for each season were created, corresponding to the thirteen weeks of each quarter of the year, amounting to a total of fifty-two verses. The author's book "The Anthroposophical Soul Calendar and the Incarnation Cycle of Man" provides a detailed information on this subject. [20]

The fourteenth stage represents the peak of the after-death development. Rudolf Steiner calls it the "great midnight hour of existence".[21] Here the human being is "set aflame" by divine powers as he nears the very source of his existence. Strengthened and enthused, he commences the work on the archetype of his future earthly body while longing for a new life on earth. He gradually descends step by step towards the earth during this process.

The twelve stages of existence between two lives on earth also find their expression in the seven-year periods of earthly life. To the best of the author's knowledge, Rudolf Steiner did not explicitly describe this mirroring in any of his lectures; at least no such lecture has been preserved. Could it be that Rudolf Steiner simply wanted to wait until he himself had reached an age to be able to speak about a greater number of seven-year periods from his own experiences? This might be the reason why he revealed the connection between the seven-year periods and the planetary spheres, shown in Figure 6 (page 26), which

---

[20] Roland Schrapp, "The Anthroposophical Soul Calendar and the Incarnation Cycle of Man", Publisher Books on Demand (BoD), Norderstedt (Germany).

[21] e.g. GA 153 "Inneres Wesen des Menschen und Leben zwischen Tod und neuer Geburt" (Inner Nature of Man, and Life between Death and New Birth), Viennese lecture cycle, or GA 205 "Menschenwerden, Weltenseele und Weltengeist – Teil I" (Man's Becoming, World Soul and World Spirit – part I).

solely covers the first sixty-three years of a human life on earth, to his audience only in 1924, after he himself had reached the age of sixty-three.

However, the twelvefold division of the earthly course of life includes further seven-year periods, which are related to the spheres of the fixed stars beyond the planetary world. Unfortunately it was not granted to Rudolf Steiner to be able to spend these seven-year periods on earth. Nonetheless, human developmental stages in the star spheres were known to him as well as the fact that human life on earth additionally shows another structure than the one described by him in the above-mentioned lectures. This is confirmed by Rudolf Steiner's lecture from 1922 about the profound wisdom of the physicians in the ancient mystery schools. Surprisingly, he spoke about the connection of the 3rd seven-year period (14 to 21 years) of human life on earth with the Sun sphere and of the 6th seven-year period (35 to 42 years) with the Saturn sphere:

"And in this way also human life must be considered. So, if an ill person between the ages of fourteen and twenty-one – this is an approximation – sought help from a physician in the mysteries, the physician knew: there are a number of diseases which simply have something to do with the passage of the person through the Sun sphere on his descent from the planetary world into the physical world. If the patient was between thirty-five and forty-two, the mystery priest knew which diseases had something to do with the person's passage through the Saturn sphere on his descent. So, he considered foremost the connection of the life on earth with the experiences of a person in the existence between death and new birth." [22]

---

[22] GA 218 "Geistige Zusammenhänge in der Gestaltung des menschlichen Organismus" (Spiritual Connections in the Formation of the Human Organism), Berlin, lecture of December 7, 1922.

This statement differs from Rudolf Steiner's sketch shown in figure 6 (page 26), based on a purely planetary view. There he assigns the 3rd seven-year period (age: 14 - 21 years) to the Venus sphere. The 6th seven-year period (age: 35 - 42 years) he assigns together with the 4th and 5th seven-year periods to the Sun sphere. In summary, he gives them the age of 21 - 42 years.

On the other hand, if one looks at the human life on earth from the point of view of the fixed stars in the sense of the twelve-fold zodiacal divisions, the correspondence of the S u n s p h e r e to the 3 r d seven-year period and of the S a t u r n s p h e r e to the 6 t h seven-year period of the earthly life comes to the fore, as given in the above quotation. This will be confirmed in the following chapters.

Before doing so, however, the question should be briefly pursued as to whether the entire human life on earth is really divided into seven-year periods or whether such a division is limited only to childhood, youth and at most the early years of the adult life.

Is the Entire Human Life on Earth Divided into Seven-Year Periods?

Anyone who has taken a closer look at Rudolf Steiner's division of human life on earth into seven-year periods will certainly have come across statements that such a division primarily applies to the first half of life, especially to the first three seven-year periods with their obvious changes in regard to the physical, mental and spiritual development of the adolescent human being. In the following seven-year periods, the differences are much less noticeable, which makes a clear delimitation more difficult. The main reason for this is that after the age of 21, further physical changes take place only very slowly and further mental and spiritual maturation is an inner process. Moreover, many people attach little importance to such further development. As young adults, they already consider themselves to be fully mature.

But even among those who would like to develop their soul and spirit, there is often little interest in examining one's own biography more closely to see whether and to what extent the years after the age of 21 still show a division into seven-year periods. Often, they only remember a few significant events, which they can no longer assign to a specific year. Of course, all this makes it difficult to discover a division into seven-year periods later in life.

In the following quote Rudolf Steiner spoke about a difference between the first and the second half of life:

"You remember that we distinguish individual periods in the life of a human being, for example, in the little booklet «The Education of the Child from the Point of View of Spiritual Science»[23]*: the period from physical birth to about the seventh year, into the time of the change of teeth, then from the seventh to about the fourteenth year, then again from about the fourteenth to the twenty-first year, periods which run roughly from seven to seven years. This division of human life into such individual periods is fairly* r e g u l a r *in the first half of a normal life. This subdivision into seven-year periods, becomes* i r r e g u l a r *in the second, in the descending half of life. The reason for this is that in relation to the first half of our life we live out those laws and actualities which are a kind of repetition of the regular course of development of mankind since primeval times, while in the second half of life we do not*

---

23 included in GA 34 "Lucifer-Gnosis 1903 – 1908".

yet live out something which has already happened in the outer world, but which will happen only in the future. Therefore, the second half of human life will become much more regular in the future than it is already today, more and more regular." [24]

For most people, then, it is true that the later life can no longer be divided so clearly and regularly into groups of seven. However, this is not necessarily the case. Individuals who thread the path of spirit discipleship, accelerate their development. The consequence of this is that what will be the case for most people "in the future", namely a regular seven-year pattern also in the second half of life, is already beginning to show in the present life on earth.

In an attempt to offer living examples of the way in which these intervals can be expressed, the author has decided, after much deliberation, to share some of his own biographical details from the second part of his life, insofar as he is in the position to assess them in retrospect. This will shed further light on why he has been able to write and publish his recently published books. Thus, rather than being the fruit of abstract thought, the extant work therefore stems from the attentive observation of his own biography.

---

[24] GA 118 "Das Ereignis der Christus-Erscheinung in der ätherischen Welt" (The Event of the Appearance of Christ in the Etheric World), Pforzheim, lecture of January 30, 1910.

Mirroring of the Higher Planes of Existence in the Earthly Course of Life

The Embryonic Life and the Moon Sphere

Human life on earth does not actually begin with birth, but with conception. It initiates a process through which the human cosmic soul-spirit being gradually unites with its future earthly body in the womb of the mother. Up to this point a human being consists of three members, namely ether body, astral body and "I". As long as the ether body is not yet occupied with the task of endowing the physical body with life processes, its second important function as a carrier of memory, comes to the fore. This quality becomes a significant experience for the human being, when he connects with the nascent physical body at the time of conception, as well as at the moment of withdrawal from it at death. This event is marked by a pictorial review of the earthly life, the so-called "life tableau", which appears as memory pictures released from the ether body of the deceased. It corresponds to a mirror-image event immediately at the beginning of a new incarnation when the human being moving into the womb of his future mother experiences a preview of his future life on earth.

"For a new incarnation, the I descends from the spiritual world with all the immortal extracts so far gained of both the etheric and the astral. It initially draws together all astral qualities to be its new astral body, qualities that reflect its development up to that point. Only then does it draw together all the etheric qualities. All this happens in the first days

after conception, and it is only from the eighteenth to the twentieth day onwards that the new ether body is working independently to develop the physical germ of the human being. Before that the maternal ether body did the things which the ether body would have to do later on. It is only on this eighteenths to twentieth day after conception that the individual who is about to incarnate and who has until then garbed its I in a new astral body and ether body, takes possession of the physical body which has so far been developed by the mother.

The moment before the possession is thus taken, the human being has exactly the same levels of existence as at the moment of death. In the latter case he has just cast off the physical body, in the former he has not yet taken up the physical body. You will therefore find it easy to understand that at the moment when the human being enters into a new physical body, something happens which is analogous to the moment when he laid it aside. At this moment he has a kind of preview of the life to come, just as at the moment of death he had a review of the past life. He will, however, forget this preview, for the constitution of the physical body is not yet such that the preview can be retained as a memory." [25]

Following the experience of the life panorama after death, the deceased soul-spiritual human being expands out into the Moon sphere. There it gradually weans itself of his lowest bodily urges and sensual desires. This process is mirrored in an analogous, though exactly reversed, process in embryonic life after conception, for the lunar forces, as rulers of all processes having to do with reproduction, are decisively involved in the formation of a new human body. This has been indicated in Figure 4 (page 18), where Rudolf Steiner assigned the "life of reproduction" to the sphere of the moon. The

[25] GA 100 "Menschheitsentwicklung und Christus-Erkenntnis" (Human Development and Knowledge of Christ), Kassel, lecture of June 23, 1907.

reproduction or procreation of earthly living beings is connected as a rule with passions and desires, that is, with the participation of forces which belong to the three lower regions of the soul world, which together form the Moon sphere (see Figure 7, page 29). Thereby the threefold structure of the cosmic human being according to body, soul and spirit is implanted into the earthly human being.

The lowest region contains the basic urges of the human body, its sensual drives and instincts. It is therefore called "region of burning desire". During the embryonic life, its forces innocently bring about the life-preserving instincts of the human being by which the foetus develops the need for food and warmth. In the womb, those needs are involuntarily satisfied. After birth, however, it becomes obvious, and above all clearly audible, how strong this drive is. The infant insistently and loudly demands that its basic needs are satisfied.

The second region contains the lowest drives of the soul, sentience and excitability. It bears the name "region of mobile sensitivity". Through this, the quality of sentience is given as well as the ability to react emotionally to external sensory stimuli.

In the third region, the lowest drives of the spirit are expressed as wishes and longings. It is therefore called the "region of wishes".[26] What is implanted here, forms the ground for longings and aspirations, which can be developed and ennobled up to high spiritual ideals.

During the sojourn in the Moon sphere after death, we are essentially occupied with ourselves. We live in images of the past earthly life. Thus, during this initial period of after-death existence, no

---

[26] GA 141 "Das Leben zwischen Tod und neuer Geburt im Verhältnis zu den kosmischen Tatsachen" (Life between Death and New Birth in Relation to the Cosmic Facts), Berlin, lecture of April 1, 1913.

social life with other deceased souls or higher spiritual beings is possible. In an analogous way, the foetus in the womb also exists within itself while sleeping and experiencing in dream images. Only in a subconscious way does the foetus sense the presence of the mother and of other family members who are expecting its birth.

The body of the embryo is surrounded by the womb during the pregnancy in a similar way as the earth is surrounded by the orbiting moon. Accordingly, in astrology the moon represents the woman and mother. In addition, the moon causes the tides in the oceans and seas of the earth. It rules over everything watery, including the amniotic fluid in which the embryo floats in the amniotic sac. It is the basis for all life processes. Thus, only in watery milieu can the seven planetary life processes be set in motion and maintained in the developing embryo.

The shape of an early embryo is nearly round. This is the time when the twelve forces of the zodiac are imprinted on it week after week sculpting the human form. As cosmic spirit-beings, which humans essentially are, they can only live in a physical body, whose form is built according to cosmic forces and laws. Rudolf Steiner once drew a sketch on the blackboard and explained it in the following way:

"If you take the human embryo and draw it according to its own lawfulness, you have to draw it out of the zodiac in this way. [...]

If you draw the zodiac in such a way, transform it in such a way, that its lawfulness reflects its relation to the earth, then one arrives at the form of the human embryo. And it is thus immediately apparent that the human embryo indeed is formed out of the whole universe, that it is a result of the universe."[27]

---

[27] GA 208 "Anthroposophie als Kosmosophie" (Anthroposophy as Cosmosophy), Dornach, lecture of October 28, 1921.

Only when the embryo has matured into a human form, which conforms to cosmic laws and forces, and has consolidated to the degree by which it can live in the solid environment and breathe air, can it become a real earthly being. Still, the neonate remains an extremely tender and sensitive creature. Its earthly human body is being structured according to the cosmic principles of the trinity (head, chest, and abdomen as expression of spirit, soul, and body), the seven-foldness of the planets (seven life processes) and according to the twelve-foldness of the zodiac or the fixed stars (twelve parts of the human form).

Figure 8: Rudolf Steiner's sketch of a human embryo

However, the three principles are not only expressed in the structure and functionality of the body, but also shape the subsequent course of life of the newly arrived citizen of the earth. How could it be otherwise when a cosmic spirit-being develops further on earth.

Figure 9 (p. 42) shows this connection between the Moon sphere and embryonic life (highlighted in gray), as well as anticipating the connection between the Mercury sphere and the first seven-year period after birth, which will be discussed in greater detail later.

Rudolf Steiner pointed also from an entirely different perspective toward the inner connection between our existence in the Moon sphere after death and the prenatal embryonic life. Namely, that if we expand into the Moon sphere after death and in the following few decades live through the experience of Kamaloka, this equals a kind of after-death embryonic period with regard to the subsequent, century-long existence between death and new birth.

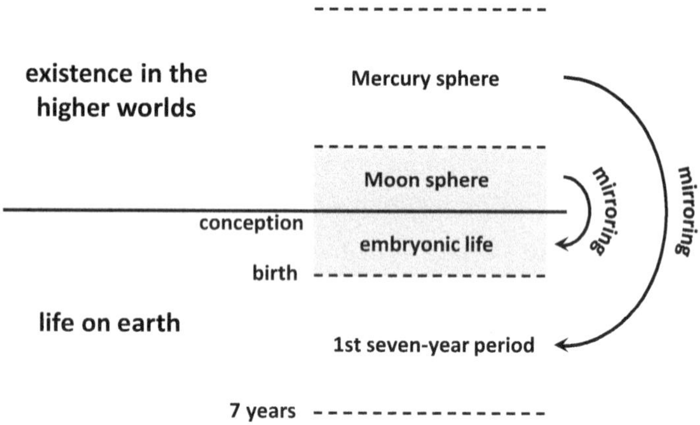

Figure 9:
Mirroring of the Moon sphere and the Mercury sphere in the course of life on earth

"Before we fully enter the physical world, we go through the embryonic period, during which the conditions of life are quite different from the moment we have fully entered the physical world as breathers of the outer air. In a certain sense, the time we pass through in the first spirit-year – the so-called Kamaloka period – is rather similar to the embryonic time. For just as a human being, as it were, seeks assistance of another to whom he entrusts himself to be carried by during ten lunar months through to the physical world, so he lets himself be carried into the spiritual world through all that holds him together with the physical world in the form of wishes and desires, from which he gradually loosens. And so is the consciousness in this first spirit year – during thirty years after death – still somewhat similar to the consciousness here in the physical world, even though the skills and the like which can only be

acquired in the physical world can only be mediated indirectly through the etheric body." [28]

Life in the womb lasts ten lunar months and thus roughly calculated almost one "earth year". According to Rudolf Steiner, the after-death transition from earthly life into the higher worlds lasts one "spirit year", which corresponds to about thirty earth years. This is how long it takes for the human being to discard the untransformed part of his astral body.

While on earth, we always experience ourselves in the centre of the world and look out to the periphery. After death we experience ourselves in the circumference and look towards the centre. All the while we move continuously along this circumference and need about 30 years until we have completed the full circle. The next period takes place on a higher level. The relationship between the centre and the periphery finds its correspondence in nature in the fact that an orbit of the earth around the sun lasts one earth year, while the period of the outermost of the traditional planets, the orbit of Saturn, lasts approximately 30 years. More accurately, Saturn's sidereal period lasts 29.5 years.

"When a person has been dead for a longer time, he has completely discarded his astral body. This happens only after decades, because the movement we complete in the spiritual world is a much slower one than the movement in the physical world. Thirty years in the spiritual world corresponds to about one year in the physical world. Man, so to speak, hurries here in the physical world. In the spiritual world he always has to go through a period with a much greater circumference than here in the physical world. In short, one year of the physical world corresponds

---

[28] GA 168 "Die Verbindung zwischen Lebenden und Toten" (The Connection between the Living and the Dead), Zürich (Switzerland), lecture of December 3, 1916.

to thirty years of the spiritual world. During the thirty years in the spiritual world one experiences approximately the same amount as during a single year in the physical world. However, one experiences more inwardly and far more intensively. [...]

While advancing through the development between death and rebirth, humans advance more slowly in order to experience everything more thoroughly. In fact, one advances in the spiritual world slower to such a degree as Saturn lags behind its movement around the sun in comparison to the earth. Saturn goes around the sun so much slower than the earth, as man moves slower in the spiritual world than here on the physical earth." [29]

According to another statement of Rudolf Steiner the Kamaloka lasts about one third of earthly life. The above calculation example with a Kamaloka duration of 30 years would therefore apply to a life span of 90 years. But even if someone lives to be "only" 80 years old, this results in almost 27 years of time in the Kamaloka, i.e. approximately the thirty years mentioned above. When working with such examples of arithmetic one must keep in mind that they illustrate only an approximate, but nevertheless real existing analogies.

---

[29] Ibidem.

The first Seven-Year Period and the Mercury Sphere (Age: 0 – 7 Years)

With the birth at the beginning of the first seven-year period the conditions for the new earth citizen change radically. The child is transferred from a watery environment to the solid earth. It sleeps and dreams itself into the earth life, similarly as the deceased sleeps and dreams himself into life after death. Only gradually do the soul-senses of the newly deceased become accustomed to the new environment. Similarly, the physical senses of the new-born need a considerable time until they can clearly perceive the outside world.

The child first gets to know its immediate environment and begins to develop an increasing attachment to it. This is the polar opposite process to the after-death experience in the Mercury sphere. There the human being has to wean himself in the reverse way of all his sensual delights and pleasures experienced in the physical world.

"The enthusiasm for nature, in so far as it has a sensual character, is subject to purification here, for example. But one must distinguish this kind of enthusiasm for nature from that higher life in nature which is of the spiritual kind and which seeks the spirit that reveals itself in the things and processes of nature. This kind of nature-sense belongs to the things which develop the spirit itself and build a lasting foundation for the spirit. This sense for nature, however, must be distinguished from deriving of pleasure which has its cause in the senses. To this end the soul needs to undergo a purification in the same way as with other inclinations which are based on mere physicality." [30]

---

[30] GA 9 "Theosophie" (Theosophy), chapter "Die drei Welten" (The three worlds), section II "Die Seele in der Seelenwelt nach dem Tode" (The soul in the soul world after death).

What we surrender after death in the Mercury sphere, namely a dependence on the earthly world of senses, is what we have to get used to again on earth in the first seven-year period to become fully functional in the sphere of the earth. In addition, we soon begin to acquire the Mercury capacities of speaking, thinking and upright walking as an expression of the innate spirit. It is through these that we rise above the animal kingdom right during the first year of life and testify that we belong to an independent higher kingdom.

The Mercury sphere belongs to the higher soul world and not to the spiritual world. In this respect it may seem strange that in the first seven-year period spiritual qualities of the human being are already coming to the fore. However, the three spheres of the higher soul world – the spheres of Mercury, Venus and Sun – are penetrated by the three spheres of the lower spiritual world – the spheres of Mars, Jupiter and Saturn. Rudolf Steiner therefore calls the higher soul world *"a kind of spiritual province of the soul region, of the soul world."*[31] The mutual interpenetration of the spheres of the soul world with spheres of the spiritual world mentioned here, will be explained in more detail later.

There is yet another connection in addition to the one here described between the Mercury sphere and the first seven-year period. Unlike during the embryonic period, where we are "isolated" within the confines of the womb, we come after birth in immediate contact with the people closest to us. Thus, we gradually develop into a social being. This happens primarily by imitating the behaviour of parents and siblings as well as close relatives and friends of the family. They become our role models, influence our social behaviour and give

---

31 GA 141 "Das Leben zwischen Tod und neuer Geburt im Verhältnis zu den kosmischen Tatsachen" (Life between Death and New Birth in Relation to the Cosmic Facts), Berlin, lecture of April 1, 1913.

us the most important inclinations towards moral or immoral impulses. Similarly, our social behaviour and our moral stance are of decisive importance for the after-death experiences in the Mercury sphere. In Rudolf Steiner's words:

"When comparing two or more individuals after death, during the period immediately following their life in Kamaloka [the Moon sphere], we find that their experiences depend on the moral constitutions which they acquired on earth. Individuals with sound moral qualities enjoy a most favourable condition in the period after the Kamaloka. Those who lack moral qualities, on the other hand, endure more challenging conditions. [...] Moreover, a moral soul disposition is rewarded by social interaction with other human spirits and with spirits of the higher hierarchies. Souls with deficient moral qualities, on the contrary, live a hermit-like life of isolation and find it extremely difficult to reach beyond the fog of their vision. This is one of the reasons for suffering after death, of feeling alone and isolated, whereas finding the connection to what is necessary, to what one needs, is an essential characteristic of sociability. And it takes a rather long time in the afterlife to pass through this sphere, which in occultism is called the Mercury sphere."[32]

Furthermore, there is an intimate connection between the ethical level of a person in the previous life on earth and his disposition for health or disease in the next life. Bad external conditions in the first seven-year period due to unfavourable karma can lead to conditions such as rickets. Also, oppressive soul experiences in early childhood, as a result of one's misconduct in the previous life, cause a disposition for illnesses. The manner in which the first seven-year period is shaped is therefore of great importance for our future state of health. Nevertheless, we should not consider diseases as karmic

---

32 Ibidem, lecture of November 5, 1912.

punishment. In reality, they help us to develop forces which are needed to overcome our moral weaknesses and bring us into harmony with the soul and spiritual world. This relationship we learn about in details in the Mercury region.

"In the Mercury region the spiritual results of illnesses are taken away from human beings. And it is there that we experience for the first time, how in the world of stars, which is essentially the world of the gods, the physical and the moral work into each other. [...] Thus, when we have passed through the gate of death and entered the Mercury region, we experience a dissolution of the spiritual effects of the diseases, see them absorbed by the spiritual beings, and the feeling arises: Now, o Gods, you have been appeased! This is an important moment in the period of life between death and rebirth. Such realities used to be known. [...] Then one knew that one can only find out what corresponds to the real nature of an illness when the truth was revealed by the Mercury beings. Therefore, all healing, all medical knowledge, was the secret of certain mysteries, the Mercury mysteries." [33]

Thus, our incarnating into the physical sense world during the first seven-year period, the development of our social behaviour and the disposition to health and illness are a true counter-image of our after-death experiences in the Mercury sphere. There we outgrow and wean ourselves from the connection with the material, physical sense world. The opposite is the case during the first seven-year period on earth when we take possession of it increasingly from year to year. In the process, the incarnating soul-spiritual human being must bring the animate physical body, which has been prepared as a "model" via the hereditary line, into harmony with itself. To what extent this succeeds

---

[33] GA 239 "Esoterische Betrachtungen karmischer Zusammenhänge – Band V" (Karmic Relationships – Vol. 5), Paris (France), lecture of May 24, 1924.

depends on the forces which one brings along from the existence between the last death and rebirth into the current earthly life. The childhood illnesses are the outward manifestation of this process. Rudolf Steiner even speaks of an "inner struggle":

"What man has as his body in the first seven years of life is simply a model to which he orients himself. Either his spiritual powers are submerged to a certain extent in what is imposed on him by the model, and he remains completely dependent on the model, or he works into the model during the first seven years of life what needs to change the model. This work, this working through, also finds its outer expression. [...] This gives rise to a struggle during the first seven years of life. From the spiritual perspective, this struggle amounts to what is outwardly expressed as symptoms in the childhood illnesses. Childhood illnesses are the expression of this inner struggle. Of course, similar forms of illness also occur in people later in life. This is the case, for example, when someone has not been able to adequately overcome the model body during the first seven years of life. Then, at a later age, an inner urge can arise to get out what has remained karmically behind. It may happen that in his twenty-eighth, twenty-ninth year of life someone is inwardly stirred to be at odds with the model more than ever before, and then he gets a childhood disease."[34]

We can see, how clearly the central aspects of the experiences in the Mercury sphere are mirrored in the first seven years of life on earth, not only in confrontation with the outer physical world, in social behaviour and interaction with other people, but also in health and illness.

If we wish to form an idea of the existence in the higher worlds, we must take into account that the transition from one sphere to the other

---

34 GA 235 "Esoterische Betrachtungen karmischer Zusammenhänge – Band I", (Karmic Relationships – Vol. I) Dornach, lecture of March 1, 1925.

does not happen abruptly as if walking through the door or across a boundary line into another set of conditions. The spheres are not so strictly separated from their neighbouring spheres as shown in a simplified way in Figure 9 (page 42) by the dashed line between the Moon sphere and the Mercury sphere. In reality, they overlap, so that each sphere projects almost halfway down into the next lower one and also almost halfway up into the next higher one. The consequence for the deceased is such that in addition to current events, one at first encounters isolated experiences of a completely different kind. After a certain period of time, these experiences move to the centre of consciousness, while the former recede into the background.

In life on earth this mutual interpenetration of neighbouring spheres is shown by the fact that the special character of a seven-year period always announces itself already in the last years of the preceding one and, after the end of the seven-year period, still works on into the first years of the following one. To the seven years of such a period belong consequently another 2 ½ to 3 preceding years and as many of the following. Therefore, we may add 2 x 2 ½ = 5 years to the number 7 and get a total of 12 years, or we add 2 x 3 = 6 years and get a total of 13 years for the effective time span of a seven-year period.

A process that has its focus in the first seven-year period, such as the encounter with earthly substances, therefore begins already in the womb and increases until birth. Disposition to illnesses due to a lack of nourishment and care, as a consequence of karmic misconduct in the previous life, can also occur during the embryonic period. The social milieu in which the mother is involved during pregnancy has an effect on the foetus in the womb as well. Thus, the forces of the Mercury sphere, which dominate the first seven-year period, radiate into the preceding embryonic life, although the latter is dominated primarily by the forces of the Moon sphere. Conversely, the forces of the Moon sphere radiate into the time after birth, for not only does the foetus depend on nourishment in the womb, but also the new-born, inasmuch as it is still suckled, requires a close physical contact with the mother or some other nurturing person. Even with the mother herself the continuing effect of the Moon forces is evident during the initial years of the first seven-year period of her child. She still produces breast milk for quite a while.

On the other hand, we can see by way of the childhood diseases how the forces of the Mercury sphere continue to work into the first two to three years of the second seven-year period, which is dominated by the forces of the Venus sphere. The occurrence of childhood diseases is therefore not limited to the first seven years of life, but extends three years further, to the age of about 10. According to Rudolf Steiner's statement on childhood diseases, quoted above, there are cases in which such diseases can occur even in later years. The cause for this is always a special karmic constellation.

In Figure 10, an attempt is made to depict the forces of the spheres working their way into their neighbouring spheres. In the upper half of the picture, the outer arrows pointing upward from the Mercury sphere indicate the upward action of the Mercury forces into the lower half of the Venus sphere. The outer arrows, which also start from the Mercury sphere and point downward, are supposed to represent the downward action of the Mercury forces into the upper half of the Moon sphere. The inner arrows in the upper half of the picture are intended to show that the forces of the Moon sphere and the Venus sphere are also working into the Mercury sphere.

Such mirroring and overlap of the planetary forces into the earthly life transpires for each of the consecutive seven-year periods.

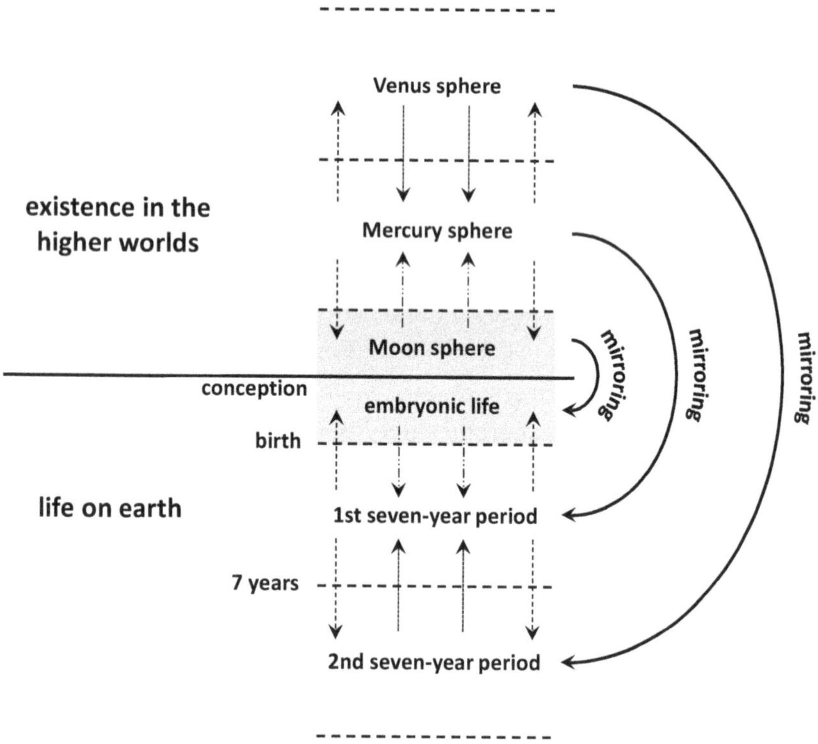

Figure 10:
Mutual penetrations of the
Moon sphere, Mercury sphere and Venus sphere
as well as their mirroring in the course of life on earth

However, it must be taken into account that during the post-mortal ascent and pre-natal descent through the higher worlds, the human being spends different lengths of time in the individual spheres. If one has acquired an affinity for a particular sphere during the earthly life or has to fulfil a specific task in the next incarnation that requires a longer sojourn in one of the spheres, then his stay there is considerably prolonged. Its influence then radiates over a longer period of the next earthly life. It is possible that the entire earthly life is given a special imprint and a corresponding basic character. In one of his Breslau lectures Rudolf Steiner gave examples of such longer after-death stays of certain individuals in the Mars, Jupiter and Saturn spheres and the resulting consequences for their next earthly incarnations. The interested reader is referred to the corresponding lecture. [35]

The second Seven-Year Period and the Venus Sphere (Age: 7 – 14 Years)

With the completion of the first seven-year period, the new earth citizen has already settled into the physical world to a certain degree. However, in order to be able to cope with all the tasks that await him in the further course of life, he will have to connect with it much more firmly. So that this does not happen unchecked and in order that he does not entirely forget in the process his origin, it is important that after seven years of settling into the physical world his attention is drawn to the existence of higher worlds from which he has only descended for a number of decades in order to gain new experiences which he can then take along to his heavenly home for further appraisal and transformation into new abilities. Therefore, religious instruction should be given right from the beginning of schooling in the transition from the first to the second seven-year period. This is particularly suitable at this age because children are still predisposed

---

[35] GA 239 "Esoterische Betrachtungen karmischer Zusammenhänge – Band V", (Karmic Relationships – Vol. 5) Breslau (formerly Germany, today called Wrocław, Poland), lecture of June 9, 1924.

to absorb and internalize everything on authority, without critical evaluation by the intellect. Moreover, during these years, many still have a certain emotional memory of their life in the higher worlds before birth.

Unfortunately, today's major world religions contain only fragments of the originally comprehensive primeval wisdom of mankind. Whoever grows up as a Hindu or Buddhist will learn a lot about the existence of higher worlds and its beings. However, he will learn nothing about the Mystery of Golgotha, through which the Christ Being has connected with mankind, and its great significance for the human evolution on earth. Those who grow up in the Christian culture, on the other hand, will learn nothing about rebirth and karma. Even the pre-existence of the soul is consistently denied and all attention is directed to the life after death. Whereby for some denominations it is doubtful whether an afterlife can even be spoken of at all. In the meantime, the original knowledge of the further development of man after death has been replaced by a mere "rest in peace", which is imagined as a long, deep sleep lasting until the "judgment day".

Those growing up in the Islamic culture are, on the one hand, imbued with religious sensitivity and insistently reminded about the continuation of life after death, however infused with imaginations of paradise modelled entirely after the earthly sense world. Such being the case, one is hardly motivated to develop "supersensory" ideas in this way. People are cured of the illusion of such a paradise already in the Mercury sphere, since it is their task there to wean themselves from everything earthly and sensual in order to live into the entirely different conditions prevailing in the higher soul world.

For the next stage of the life after death, however, it is of great importance whether a person has developed a religious mood and devotion to the divine in his soul during his life on earth. For the after-death stay in the Venus sphere this is of similar central importance as the social behaviour and moral level of a person for the Mercury sphere. It is therefore extremely regrettable if someone, as it is unfortunately widespread today, as a result of turning to a purely materialistic worldview in the course of his life on earth, comes to reject the very possibility of the existence of higher worlds and entities. Rudolf Steiner described quite clearly the consequences of such an inner attitude and how it affects the experiences in the Venus sphere:

"After having passed through the Mercury sphere, as it is called in occultism, we experience in another period the so-called V e n u s s p h e r e, we feel ourselves as inhabitants of Venus. It is here, between Mercury and Venus, [...] where the beings of the higher hierarchies can approach the human being. But now it depends again on whether we have made ourselves ready in the right way to be accepted as sociable spirits into the ranks of the hierarchies, to be able to have something to do with them, or whether we will only know of their presence, but have to pass by them like hermits, as it were, and be loaners in the spiritual world. And in this Venus sphere it depends again on something else whether we are sociable spirits or lonely wandering spirits. Whereas in the previous sphere it is only possible to be a sociable spirit if we have prepared ourselves by acquiring morality here on earth, the force which gives us access to sociability, that is, to a certain social life in the Venus sphere, is essentially the religious life, the religious mood of the soul. And we can most certainly condemn ourselves to be hermits in the Venus sphere if we have not developed a religious mood during earthly life, a feeling of our belonging together with the Infinite, with the Divine. Yes, this is indeed the case which presents itself to occult observation, namely that individuals lock themselves up into the prison of their own by

atheistic disposition, by rejecting any relationship of their finite self to the infinity." [36]

If someone has developed a religious mood in the previous life on earth, he will not only be allowed to lead a "sociable life" in the Venus sphere, but will also have created conditions which allow him to take part in religious instruction as a child in the next life during his second seven-year period in which the experiences of the Venus sphere are mirrored. It is even possible that as a result of the religious mood of his soul in the previous life he will already receive a religiously oriented education in the three years before the beginning of the second seven-year period, at the pre-school age, or he will even be admitted to a church-based kindergarten and will be introduced in a pictorial narrative way to supernatural ideas.

With the beginning of school lessons in the transition to the second seven-year period, children with Christian cultural background usually participate in denominational religious instruction. If they are Catholic, they are familiarized with the church ritual and are prepared for the first Holy Communion. Towards the end of the same seven-year period, the Confirmation marks a certain conclusion of religious instruction for Catholics and Protestants. Often the religious mood radiates far into the third seven-year period. Some children who have been raised Catholic even feel moved to assist as servers at the altar. The reason for this may be a closer connection with the church cultus already in the previous incarnation. For some, the desire to study theology already arises in their youth. This naturally causes a closer connection with the Venus sphere and a longer stay in it during life after death.

---

[36] GA 141 "Okkulte Untersuchungen über das Leben zwischen Tod und neuer Geburt" (Occult Investigations into the Life between Death and New Birth), Berlin, lecture of November 26, 1912.

As an illustration, the author would like to share an insight from his own biography. He grew up in a Catholic home and was sent as a boy to a parochial kindergarten run by the "Franciscan Nuns of the Divine Heart of Jesus"[37]. They are also known as "Gengenbach Sisters" because their priory is located in the town of Gengenbach in Baden-Württemberg[38]. On occasion, one of the nuns would gather the children and show them large picture panels with scenes from the Old and New Testaments. She would then describe the pictures in the most vivid way. For us children, this was always very impressive and moving.

In the case of the author, the religious mood was additionally reinforced by the fact that from the age of 7 - 14 he was mainly cared for by his Catholic grandmother, with whom he would often read Bible stories in the evenings. When one day a friend of the grandparents came for visit and asked the boy "What do you want to be when you grow up?", the child blurted "A priest", to the horror of his atheist-minded grandfather. However, this wish vanished soon enough already during the same seven-year period, because the local pastor was a rather rude man. Many children were downright afraid of him. In the case of the author, the experiences associated with this led in the course of his second seven-year period to an important realization, namely, that Christianity and churchianity are two very different things. Thus, the way opened for him to cultivate a religious feeling beyond the narrow borders of his religious denomination.

Under the influence of the Venus sphere and its beings, an entirely different development likewise takes place during the second seven-year period. The life processes in the human organism are an

---

[37] A Roman Catholic religious community of the "Regulated Third Order of St. Francis of Assisi."

[38] a federal state in the South West of Germany

expression of the activity of the etheric body. The latter also governs the development of the glandular function. In particular the sex glands now reach maturity and become active. They serve the "seventh life activity", the reproductive life. As a result, teenagers reach sexual maturity at the age of 14 ± 3 years. Of course, there are, karmically conditioned exceptions as is the case in premature or delayed puberty.

The third Seven-Year Period and the Sun Sphere (Age: 14 – 21 Years)

Around the age of fourteen, the immortal soul-spiritual human being, descending from higher worlds, unites more intimately with the earthly body than was possible during the earlier childhood years. The astral body can now unfold its effect more freely and the individuality begins to be more clearly noticeable from within as noted in the tendency towards emancipation from the family and from its prevailing opinions. This soul process is of great importance and points to the adolescent's forming of his or her own judgements and independence. The teen is well on the way becoming an adult.

Through diverse and increasingly comprehensive education, new interests are developed and the view of the world widens. From the age of 14 ± 3 years, many religious young adults feel motivated to look beyond the limits of their own religious denomination. The fact that there are other ways of looking at the divine attracts attention; be it doctrines of the gods of the past, such as those of the ancient Greeks, Romans, Egyptians and Germanic peoples, or the teachings of the great contemporary world religions outside of Christianity. This special kind of soul development in the third seven-year period is based on an influence from the Sun sphere which now comes into effect.

Individuals who partook in far-reaching and impressive experiences in the Sun sphere after death and one more time before rebirth, feel clearly the new impulse which transcends nations and religions, encompassing even the whole of humanity.

"The next thing that man experiences after the Venus sphere is the S u n s p h e r e. As soul beings, we actually become sun dwellers between death and the new birth. For the Sun sphere, however, something else is necessary than for the Venus sphere. For the Sun sphere there is the clear, the eminent necessity, if we want to prosper in it between death and the new birth, not merely to understand a certain group of people, but to understand all human souls, to be able to gain, as it were, points of contact with all souls. And in the Sun sphere we already feel as hermits, as lonely ones, if we are constricted by the prejudices of some religious denomination and are not able to understand the one whose soul is steeped in another denomination. Those, for example, wo have developed on earth appreciation only for their own religious denomination, do not understand – as we may say now – the followers of any denomination, during their sojourn in the Sun sphere. However, this non-understanding is unlike here on earth. Here, people can walk side by side without any soul-understanding of the other. They can divide into different religious beliefs and world views. Since we not only all extend to the Sun sphere, but interpenetrate each other, we form a union there a n d yet are separated by our inner being. There, every separation and non-understanding is a source of terrible suffering. The encounter with those of other religious denominations can become a heavy burden and the cause of an unbridgeable reproach, if we haven't educated ourselves accordingly on earth. [...]

When St. Paul wrested the Christian belief in Christ Jesus from the mere Judaism and said: «Christ died not only for the Jews but also for the Gentiles», he did a great deed for the right understanding of Christianity. For it would be quite erroneous if someone wanted to claim that the

Mystery of Golgotha took place only for those who call themselves Christians. It was accomplished for all humanity! This is also what St. Paul means when he says that Christ died also for the Gentiles, not only for the Jews. For what has passed into all earthly life through the Mystery of Golgotha also has significance for all earthly life. And as grotesque as it may sound still today to those who do not make the distinction that is about to be made, it must be said: He only understands the root of Christianity who, for example, is able to look at a follower of another religious system – regardless of whether he calls himself Indian, Chinese or something else – in such a way that he asks himself: How much Christianity is in him?" [39]

In another lecture Rudolf Steiner described the profound knowledge of the physicians in the ancient mystery schools. Here he pointed out a connection between the pre-birth sojourn in the Sun sphere and the third seven-year period of the following life on earth, that is the age from 14 to 21 years:

"And in this way also human life must be considered. So, if an ill person between the ages of fourteen and twenty-one – this is an approximation – sought help from a physician in the mysteries, the physician knew: there are a number of diseases which simply have something to do with the passage of the person through the Sun sphere on his descent from the planetary world into the physical world. [...] So, he considered foremost the connection of the life on earth with the experiences of a person in the existence between death and new birth." [40]

---

[39] GA 141 "Das Leben zwischen dem Tode und der neuen Geburt im Verhältnis zu den kosmischen Tatsachen" (Life between the Death and the New Birth in Relation to the Cosmic Facts), Berlin, lecture of Nov. 20, 1912.

[40] GA 218 "Geistige Zusammenhänge in der Gestaltung des menschlichen Organismus" (Spiritual Connections in the Formation of the Human Organism), Berlin, lecture of December 7, 1922.

This statement by Rudolf Steiner from the year 1922 proves that already two years before he gave a lecture at the age of 63, describing the seven-year periods from a planetary point of view and writing a seven-part sketch on the blackboard (figure 6, page 26), he certainly had knowledge about the fact that there is another way of assigning the seven-year periods to the spheres, which is based on the stellar point of view and consequently also takes into account the spheres belonging to the fixed stars.

In what way did the influence of the Sun sphere in the third seven-year period make itself felt in the author of the present book? Like many of his contemporaries, he became intensely interested in the mythology and legends of the ancient Greeks, Romans, Egyptians, and Germanic tribes. He even made drawings of the most important Greco-Roman gods in order to depict them as vividly as he saw them in his imagination.

Soon after, he turned to the contemporary world religions, Hinduism, Buddhism, Judaism, and Islam, with the first two being of greatest interest. The eastern doctrine of rebirth and karma made a deep impression and a great deal of sense to him and offered the only reasonable explanation for observable events in daily life. Only in this way could the different living conditions of people and their strokes of destiny be reconciled with the existence of an all-loving supreme God. In this regard, he felt it was fortunate that his high school religious class was interdenominational. By way of the new Protestant religion teacher, he learned, on the one hand, about views that tended to deny the divine nature of Jesus Christ, regarding him simply as a highly moral human being, perhaps a revolutionary, but ultimately the "simple man from Nazareth" to whom the Protestant theological research of the 19th century had already reduced him. On the other hand, the religion teacher was quite open to the author's wish to deal with the other world religions in the classroom, a request to which the majority of the class readily agreed. This indicates that a similar feeling lived also in other classmates, and that they also felt, though unconsciously, the effect of their prenatal stay in the Sun sphere. Needless to say, at the time, none of us had any inkling about the above statements of Rudolf Steiner.

Looking back at the first four sections of the life on earth, it is apparent that the after-effects from the spheres of the soul world surfaced in them in exactly the reverse order of the prenatal descent, as it is typical for mirroring. The Moon sphere characteristically encompasses the three regions of the lower soul world as well as a transitional region, so that the passage through them is condensed in time compared to the duration of stay in the following spheres, which correspond to diverse regions. This could be related to the embryonic life, in which the entire biological evolution of the human being is telescoped within several months and thus also condensed in time. The connection to the Moon sphere is likewise evident in that the modern-day physicians calculate the duration of a pregnancy in lunar months, based on the lunar cycle.

From birth on, the prenatal experiences from the spheres of the higher soul world are mirrored in the first three seven-year periods of life on earth. As a consequence, a spiritual influence is already noticeable, albeit indirectly at first via the soul world. As mentioned, Rudolf Steiner calls the higher soul world *"a kind of spiritual province of the soul region, of the soul world".* [41] Man is indeed a spirit-being who, in the course of childhood and adolescence, settles in his new earthly body, belabours it, and prepares it for the task of serving him as a bodily vehicle. Figure 11 offers an overview of this process.

---

[41] GA 141 "Das Leben zwischen Tod und neuer Geburt im Verhältnis zu den kosmischen Tatsachen" (Life between Death and New Birth in Relation to the Cosmic Facts), Berlin, lecture of April 1, 1913.

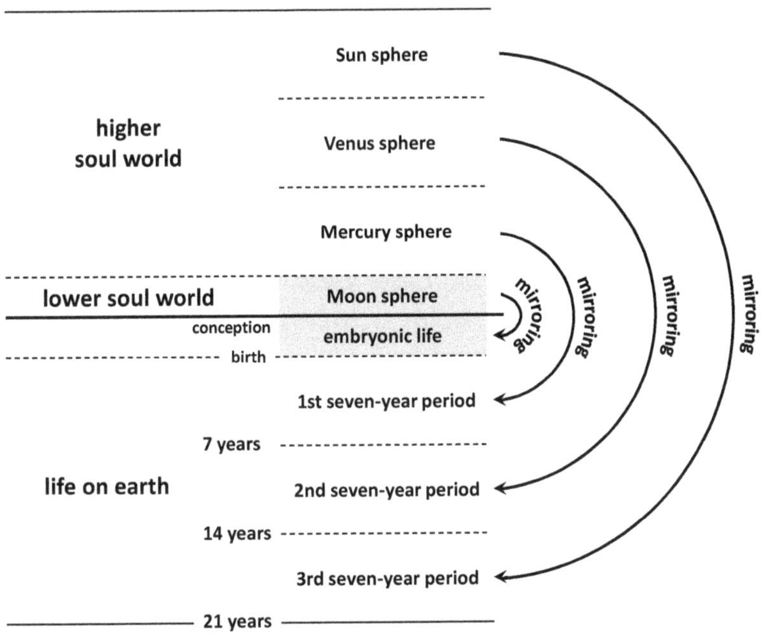

Figure 11:
Mirroring of the spheres of the lower and higher soul world in the course of life on earth

The 4th Seven-Year Period and the Mars Sphere (Age: 21 – 28 Years)

The tasks of the first three seven-year periods of life on earth are to develop the bodily organization of man to the extent that it can become the bearer of an "I". This requires a corresponding preparation of those members of being which man has in common with the other kingdoms of nature on earth: the physical body, the etheric or life body, and the astral or soul body. Rudolf Steiner has summarized this necessary series of development as follows:

"The physical body has its especial development in the first seven years of life. We perceive further that in the second seven years of life, from the change of teeth until sexual maturity, the forces of the etheric body play in man. Then the forces of the astral body begin to play, and only later, about the 20th or 21st year (depending on his whole organization and on the nature of the forces in him), begins what appears in man as the 'I', as the bearer of the I, with that force which it really has because of its organization for the whole life of man as the bearer of the I. That the bearer of the I first becomes really capable of living in the 20th or 21st year is not often observed in our present time, because we are not yet inclined to pay attention to these things. [...] Only around the 20th year does man develop his forces in such a way that a completely self-supporting I-bearer now exists. Earlier this I-bearer is not yet developed; earlier the human corporeality, even the super-sensible, is not yet a proper I-bearer. So if we consider the members of man in the light of the great world-principle, we must say that, through the peculiarities of his organization, man is really ripe to develop an I out of himself only in his 20th or 21st year, not earlier." [42]

The I is a spiritual member of the human being, and as such it needs forces from the spheres of the spirit world for its development. A special influx of such forces into the earthly course of life begins approximately from the 21st year of life. This marks the point in time from which on, in addition to the influences from the soul world, those from the spiritual world intervene directly. Man thus becomes a spirit-

[42] GA 143 "Erfahrungen des Übersinnlichen – Die drei Wege der Seele zu Christus" (Experiences of the Supernatural – The Three Ways of the Soul to Christ), Stockholm (Sweden), lecture of April 16, 1912.

being on earth not only fully conscious of himself but also fully responsible for his deeds.[43]

Human development during the next three seven-year periods is analogous to that of the first three periods. Much like in the first seven-year period, in the 4th seven-year period, at the age of 21 to 28, the focus is initially on the physical-sentient. During this period we are very receptive to all kinds of sensations that the sensory stimuli trigger in our soul. That is why Rudolf Steiner says that we primarily develop the sentient soul during these years of life on earth.

At birth we are separated from the mother to have an independent bodily existence. Similarly, when we reach adulthood, we detach ourselves from the family as an independent individuality. A second, now soul-spiritual, "cutting the cord" takes place. This process is accompanied by the fact that most young adults leave the parental home during the course of the 4th seven-year period and find a home of their own. For some, this may be just a room in a shared student flat or student residence, while others instead rent their own apartment right away or move in with their life partner. Others, still, start their own family, which once again makes the bodily the foremost concern. Even those who continue to live in their parents' home feel the need in this seven-year period to design their room more according to their own individuality and perhaps to include the room of a sibling who has already moved out in their little "kingdom". No matter in which way the emancipation from the parents may take place, the process is an image of sort of the physical separation of the new-born from the womb.

---

[43] In Germany, when a person reaches the age of 18, he or she acquires full legal right and is considered an adult. From the point of view of criminal law, however, it is verified, until the age of 21, whether juvenile criminal law must be applied or whether the maturity of an adult has been reached, whereupon a judgment must be made according to adult criminal law.

The deeper reason for this striking inner resemblance of the first seven-year period with the 4th seven-year period lies in the mutual penetration of those spheres which are mirrored in these two periods. As has already been shown in figure 10 (page 52), each sphere reaches half-way into the respective neighbouring spheres. However, in addition to the former, there is another interpenetration. For example, each sphere of the "higher soul world" is also penetrated by a certain sphere of the "lower spiritual world". This is illustrated in Figure 12, where the respective spheres are shown side by side. The Mercury sphere, the lowest sphere of the "higher soul world", is penetrated by the Mars sphere, the lowest sphere of the "lower spiritual world". Rudolf Steiner, therefore referred to the sphere of Mercury in the following way: *"On approaching the Mercury sphere, however, the soul encounters what is described in my «Theosophy» as a kind of spiritual province of the soul region, of the soul world."*[44] Here, the influence of the spiritual world already reaches into the soul world. In the same way the Venus sphere is penetrated by the Jupiter sphere and the Sun sphere by the Saturn sphere.

When the human being expands and enters the Moon sphere after death, his first task is to wean himself from the missing physical body and from all the desires that have been aroused through it in his astral body and which can only be satisfied by physical means.

With the transition into the Mercury sphere, this task of weaning extends to all ideas and wishes that still are somehow related to a physical external world. Our new external world is then the soul world, which is astral in nature. In it we relive the unconscious

---

44 GA 141 "Das Leben zwischen Tod und neuer Geburt im Verhältnis zu den kosmischen Tatsachen" (Life between Death and New Birth in Relation to the Cosmic Facts), Berlin, lecture of April 1, 1913.

experiences which we passed through during the periods of deep sleep while on earth. Those experiences, however, are relived in reverse order. When we have arrived at the beginning of our earthly life, in our earliest childhood, we are allowed to move from the temporal regions of the soul world into the timeless regions of the spiritual world, in the full sense of Christ's words: *"Truly, I tell you, unless you are converted and become like little children, you will not enter into the kingdom of heaven."* (Matthew 18:3 / Mark 10:15).

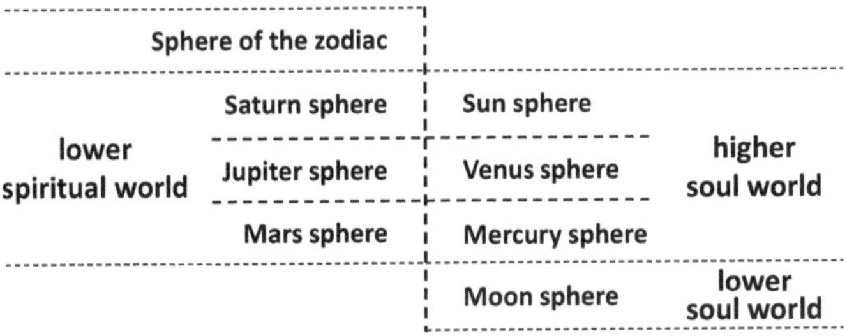

Sphere of the zodiac
Saturn sphere
Sun sphere
lower spiritual world
Jupiter sphere
Venus sphere
higher soul world
Mars sphere
Mercury sphere
Moon sphere
lower soul world

Figure 12: Mutual penetration of the planetary spheres of the lower spiritual world with those of the higher soul world

The entry into the Mars sphere of the spiritual world takes place in such a way that our perception for its beings and forces opens up. There, we encounter the spiritual archetypes of all that we have experienced on earth in the outer, inanimate world. Thus, the Mercury sphere of the soul world and the Mars sphere of the spiritual world open up for us a new outer world.

When, in the first seven-year period of life on earth, the child settles into the earthly outer world, initially into the family environment, this also is going on under the influence of forces from the Mercury sphere. In the 4th seven-year period, one becomes a member of the wider community and takes part in public life and in the world at large under the influence of forces from the Mars sphere. As a responsible adult one is given the task to provide for one's own material basis through professional activity or at least to work towards this goal by way of vocational training or study.

Even when unaware of the fact that forces from the planetary spheres have a decisive influence on our earthly life and on our soul-spiritual development, this is nevertheless the case. In reality, we are cosmic beings, who are not only in our form and life-functions influenced by the forces of the planetary and stellar worlds, but also in the successive stages of our soul-spiritual development throughout the earthly course of life.

"On earth we live between birth and death. Between death and new birth the human being is in a certain connection with the other planets. You will find described in my «Theosophy» the Kamaloka. This sojourn of man in the [lower] soul world is a time during which he becomes a Moon-dweller. Then he becomes a Mercury-dweller, then a Venus-dweller, then a Sun-dweller, Mars-dweller, Jupiter-dweller, Saturn-dweller, and then a dweller in the wider celestial or world space. One does not speak incorrectly when one says that between two incarnations on earth there are embodiments on other planets, spiritual embodiments. Today man is not yet so far in his development that he can remember in his incarnation what he has experienced between death and new birth, but in the future this will be possible. Even if he cannot remember now what he has experienced on Mars, for example, he still has the powers of Mars within him, even if he doesn't know anything

about it. One can certainly say: Now I am an Earth-dweller, but the powers within me include something that I acquired on Mars." [45]

After Rudolf Steiner had spoken these words in his lecture, he referred to Copernicus, Galileo, and Giordano Bruno as examples of people who brought their abilities for their earthly deeds, with which they essentially shaped the modern scientific-materialistic world view, from the Mars sphere. However, not only them, but all of us are influenced by such world view today and direct our thoughts primarily to the physical. We have acquired this tendency and ability during the post-mortal and pre-natal sojourn in the Mars sphere.

"And so it is with the whole of mankind. That people think like Copernicus or Giordano Bruno is due to the Mars forces they acquired between death and a new birth. "

A subconscious memory of the prenatal soul-spiritual existence between two incarnations in the universe surrounding the earth is the deeper reason why scientifically oriented people today feel a real longing to send space probes to other planets, to look with telescopes into the depths of space, even to colonize other planets. In the last decade, not coincidentally, the desire to soon send humans specifically to Mars and prepare it for colonization by part of humanity has come to the fore among many astronomers and laymen interested in astronomy. The materialistic justification for this is certainly the fact that Mars comes very close to the Earth every two years and is most similar to it. From the occult point of view, however, this is based on an emotional memory, working in the subconscious, of the after-death and pre-natal bodiless existence in the spiritual Mars sphere, which is

---

[45] GA 130 "Das esoterische Christentum und die geistige Führung der Menschheit" (Esoteric Christianity and the Spiritual Guidance of Humanity), Neuchâtel (Switzerland), lecture of December 18, 1912.

so decisive especially for our times. Here again the spiritual is mirrored in the physical.

After all, many of us have a distinct feeling that the real home of the human being is the cosmos. However, we tend to project the subconscious memories of our existence in the cosmos between two incarnations onto the material cosmos instead of relating them to the supernatural soul-spiritual cosmos, which underlies the outer, material appearance of the planetary and starry world.

In earlier ages, according to Rudolf Steiner, people in their earthly lives came under the stimulating influence not only of the Mars sphere, but also of even higher spheres of the spiritual world, in a completely natural way, simply by growing older.

"It turned out to me that mankind in the first post-Atlantean culture period, the primeval Indian, was in a certain age, however, in an age which cannot be compared with youth, but which can be compared with the individual human age from the fifty-sixth to the forty-ninth year of life. [...] Then follows the primeval Persian cultural period. There mankind, by developing itself further, goes through an age, which now, if one wants to compare it with an age of the individual, corresponds to that from the forty-ninth to the forty-second year of life. Man grows older, mankind grows younger. The Egyptian period must be compared in the individual man with the age between the forty-second and thirty-fifth year of life. The Greco-Roman period must be compared to the age of the individual between the thirty-fifth and twenty-eighth years of life, and the present fifth post-Atlantean cultural period is comparable to the age of man from the twenty-eighth to the twenty-first years. And if we ask: How old is the present humanity? – we must answer: it has an age of about twenty-seven years. And only then can one understand all that has

taken place within mankind, if one lets this strange mystery of evolution come before one's soul. For this is how things really are." [46]

The 28th and 27th years of life are years which belong to the 4th seven-year period, which is connected with the Mars sphere. And because this sphere contains the spiritual archetypes only of everything inanimate physical, purely material, today's mankind shows such a strong inclination to materialism and such a striking lack of understanding for everything living, soulful or even spiritual. A purely physically oriented natural science has become predominant under the influence of Mars, which denies life, as well as the soul and the spirit, an independent existence from the body.

Mars, however, did not always have this effect. Our development in the Mars sphere reached a low point in the 15th century, at the beginning of the fifth cultural epoch. Since then, most of us still bring from Mars the inclination to a purely physical, scientific world view into the earth life. Conversely, there are people who turn away from this development, and at times even develop a strong aversion not only against materialism, but against everything material in general. They strive for an ascetic life strictly detached from the world. It is into these two kinds that humanity threatens to split. This danger called for the intervention by the spiritual leadership of the human evolution. Therefore, already towards the end of the 16th century, Christian Rosenkreutz, the leading Christian master of our time, called together a larger circle of incarnated and discarnate souls, collaborating on the human evolution, to a conference, in which he pointed to this ominous future perspective. According to Rudolf Steiner, his words ran something like:

---

46 GA 174a "Mitteleuropa zwischen Ost und West" (Central Europe between East and West), Munich, lecture of May 19, 1917.

"Let us look at the future of the world. The world is moving fast in the direction of practical activities, industry, railways, and so on. Human beings will become like beasts of burden. And those who do not want this will be, like Francis of Assisi, impractical with regard to life, and they will turn to the inner life only. Christian Rosenkreutz made it clear to his listeners that there was no way on earth of preventing the formation of these two classes of men. Despite all that might be done for them between birth and death, nothing could hinder mankind being divided into these two classes. As far as conditions on the earth were concerned it is impossible to find a remedy for the division into these two classes. Help can only come if a kind of education could be brought about that did not take place between birth and death but between death and a new birth." [47]

Human beings need both tendencies in their development, turning towards the earth as well as away from the earth. In life after death, turning away from the earth is beneficial from the Mars sphere onwards, the lowest sphere of the spiritual world, where it should even be developed quite intensively. For this purpose, Buddha was to give the Mars culture, which had reached its lowest point, a new impulse in order to ascend, through his teaching of love and compassion, and thus create the prerequisite for turning away from the earth and turn towards the spirit in the right way, in order to enable us to perform our tasks on earth in a sufficiently spirit-filled way, without sinking into materialism. This was decided in agreement with Buddha at the second conference of Christian Rosenkreutz with the spiritual leaders of mankind. In Rudolf Steiner's words from the same lecture:

---

[47] GA 130 "Das esoterische Christentum und die geistige Führung der Menschheit" (Esoteric Christianity and the Spiritual Guidance of Humanity), Neuchâtel (Switzerland), lecture of December 18, 1912.

"And it was announced at this [second] conference that the being who incarnated as Gautama Buddha, as the spiritual being he now was since becoming «Buddha», would transfer the scene of his activities to Mars. The individuality of Gautama Buddha was, as it were, sent by Christian Rosenkreutz from the earth to Mars. So Gautama Buddha leaves the scene of his activity and goes to Mars, and in the year 1604 the individuality of Gautama Buddha accomplished for Mars a deed similar to what the Mystery of Golgotha was for the earth. [...]

Nothing less was accomplished than that the possibility was given of averting from humanity the threatened separation into two classes, so that humanity might remain united. And t h o s e w h o w a n t t o d e v e l o p e s o t e r i c a l l y despite their absorption in practical life can achieve their goal because the Buddha is working from Mars and not from the earth, so that also the forces which help to promote a h e a l t h y e s o t e r i c l i f e come from the activity of Buddha. In my book «Knowledge of the Higher Worlds and Its Attainment», I have dealt with the methods that are appropriate for m e d i t a t i o n today. The essential point is that in Rosicrucian training, development is such that the human being is not torn away from the earthly activities demanded of him by his karma. Rosicrucian esoteric development is compatible with any kind of situation or occupation in life. [...]

Through the deed of redemption performed by Gautama Buddha on Mars, it became possible for us, when we are passing through our period of development on Mars between death and rebirth, to become followers of Francis of Assisi without causing subsequent deprivation to the earth. Grotesque as it may seem, it is nevertheless true that since the seventeenth century every human being is a buddhist, a franciscan, an immediate follower of Francis of Assisi for a time, whilst he is on Mars. Francis of Assisi has subsequently only had one brief incarnation on earth as a child; and he died in childhood and has not incarnated since.

From then onwards he has been connected with the work of Buddha on Mars and is one of his most eminent followers."

In a lecture in Stuttgart Rudolf Steiner continued on the same subject:

"If we go back to earlier centuries, we find that the forces radiated from Mars which inspired men to that which human beings needed in earlier times: physical forces, to further the evolution of mankind. It is not merely a myth but an occult truth that what has developed as warlike force and warlike complication in the world, what has made man energetic, courageous through centuries and millennia, stems from an influx of the forces of Mars. But such is the life of a planet that its forces go through an ascending and a descending development. And Mars has changed in a certain way its mission during the last centuries. The warlike forces that are developed still now are the ebbing warlike life of the previous centuries; [...]

That which had always emanated from Mars, and was part of its essence, that very thing the Buddha transformed by his sacrifice. He transformed the whole nature and essence of Mars. For Mars, the Buddha has become the great Redeemer. It was a sacrifice of him. You only have to remember how the Buddha arose to the doctrine or message of universal peace, of harmonious existence. He was then transferred into that planetary sphere from which the force of aggressiveness originated. He, the Prince of Peace, crucified himself, so to speak, though not through the Mystery of Golgotha. In this way, something else is brought into the Mars sphere: Mars is permeated by the being of the Buddha. As on earth the substance of the Christ has flowed out from the Mystery of Golgotha, so the peace substance of the Buddha flows into the Mars sphere, and since then is in the Mars sphere." [48]

---

[48] GA 140 "Okkulte Untersuchungen über das Leben zwischen Tod und neuer Geburt" (Occult Investigations on Life between Death and New Birth), Stuttgart, lecture of February 17, 1913.

Our stay in the spheres of the spiritual world extends over centuries. Therefore, the new Mars forces transformed by Buddha could be brought into earthly life by reincarnating human souls only from the 19th century onwards, albeit quite sparingly at first. In the future, however, all spiritually oriented people will be able to absorb these new Buddha impulses of peace, compassion and tolerance as they pass through the Mars sphere.

"At present the ability to receive such talents is still limited among human beings because it is only comparatively recently that the Buddha accomplished the Mystery on Mars. In future, human souls will be more and more capable of receiving forces from the Buddha in the Mars sphere. But in the nineteenth century there were already some personalities — and this was disclosed to those able to perceive it — who were able to develop their faculties here on earth as a result of the influences they received from Buddha through their passage in the Mars sphere. The course of life between death and rebirth is indeed complex and wonderful." [49]

We, as spiritually oriented people, had highly significant experiences during our last stay in the Mars sphere. They are mirrored precisely in the 4th seven-year period of our present life on earth. The intensity with which this happens depends mainly on two conditions. First, on the degree of consciousness which we could maintain after our last death up to the Mars sphere. This, in turn, depended on whether we had already developed a kinship with the Mars sphere in our previous life on earth by taking an interest in the spiritual foundations of the physical world. However, there is a second requirement, which is also a condition for an encounter with the exalted Buddha in the Mars sphere. According to a strict cosmic law,

---

49 Ibidem, Frankfurt, lecture of March 2, 1913.

we can make contact in life after-death only with people whom we have already met in one of our earth lives.

"If the bond between man to man could not be tied on earth, it could not be tied in the spirit realm either. The unions that exist between man and man are such that they are formed here and then continue in the spiritual world. But we can never form them with human beings who are somehow predestined to be embodied on earth if we have the opportunity to get to know them on earth but do not use it. What we have missed here, we cannot replace in the spiritual world in the time we are living through between death and rebirth." [50]

Therefore, all those who never met the Buddha on earth in one of his previous incarnations as a Bodhisattva, or in his last incarnation in which he ascended to the loftiness of Buddhahood, could never meet him in the spirit world either, unless they could rise consciously from earth into the spirit world as highly developed spirit disciples. Hence an assistance was necessary, since the meeting with Buddha in the Mars sphere is of extraordinary importance for humanity, because through it harmony, compassion, love, and striving for peace are strengthened, all that which Buddha already initiated on earth. Whoever, during life on earth, joins inwardly with Christ, Who remains connected with us as the Risen One until the end of earthly times, whoever absorbs the Christ-impulse in himself on earth, will be given the opportunity to meet the Buddha in the Mars sphere, even if this will be the first encounter with him for the person concerned.

"And even if it is impossible for the ordinary person to meet people in the spiritual regions with whom he has not established a relationship here, it is nonetheless possible between death and rebirth that the earthly man who has received the Christ-impulse here, who has

---

[50] Ibidem.

permeated himself with it, will at least meet the Buddha over there, although he will not meet other people with whom he did not get in touch with here. [..]

Unless man is able to take with him the light to illumine his experience between death and rebirth, he stumbles in the dark. This also holds good for this exceptional case. A person who departs from the earth through the gate of death without having taken the Christ impulse into himself, who wished to know nothing of it, will not have the slightest intimation of the influences of Buddha during his next life in the spiritual world as he passes through the Mars sphere. For him it is as if the Buddha were not present. It should be borne in mind that we encounter the beings of the Higher Hierarchies, but whether or not we perceive them and establish the necessary connection with them depends on whether we kindled a light in our last earthly existence so that we do not pass them by and are able to receive impulses from them. That is why it is a complete fallacy to maintain that it is unnecessary to concern oneself with the beyond during earthly existence." [51]

In addition to the Buddhists, since 1604 all those Christians can meet the Buddha in the Mars sphere who took up the Christ impulse at the latest in their last incarnation in the Middle Ages, even if they have never met the Buddha directly in an earthly life before. For many of them, the forces they absorb in the Mars sphere will initially still remain in the subconscious and only permeate their emotional life. This can manifest itself in the most varied ways, such as someone being drawn to Buddhism. Probably this is the reason for the fact that within the Christian West so many people have turned to Buddhism in the last decades.

---

51 Ibidem.

Many others bring with them a commitment to peace on earth as a result of experiencing the effect of Buddha's act of salvation on Mars.

Spirit-oriented individuals will develop an increasing interest in meditation, Christian Rosenkreutz, or esoteric Christianity in their 4th seven-year period, some perhaps already in the last three years of the preceding period.

Still others may feel very intensely the love for animals of Francis of Assisi and therefore change their diet to vegetarian or even vegan. The latter, which dispenses completely with dairy products, has now become a real fashion. Rudolf Steiner, however, expressly warns against this, whereas he recommends a vegetarian diet, which includes dairy products, as beneficial for the spiritually striving.

"It will mean a real relief for the whole development of human life if people can abstain from eating meat. On the other hand, certain misgivings begin to arise if a person wants to be a fanatical vegetarian in the sense that he wants to avoid all milk and all dairy products. Particularly in the case of development of the soul towards the spiritual, this can involve certain dangers, for the reason that a person, by avoiding milk and milk-product consumption, very easily adopts an attitude of striving away from the earth and therefore losing the threads that connect him with the earthly human needs and tasks..

It should therefore be noted that in a certain sense it is good if the anthroposophical aspirant does not turn himself into a fanatical spiritual enthusiast by creating difficulty for the physical sheath by adding to what already wants to take him away from all the kinship with the earthly-human. So, in order that we do not become eccentrics with excessive striving for soul development, and thus become alienated from human feeling and human activity on earth, it is beneficial, if we, as wanderers on earth, let ourselves be weighed down in a certain way by the consumption of milk and of dairy products.

And it can even be a quite systematic training for a person not only to live always in the spiritual worlds, so to speak, and thereby to become alienated from the earth, but also to fulfil his tasks on the earth. It can be a systematic training not to be a mere vegetarian, but to enjoy milk and dairy products, too. Thereby he will make his organism, his physical sheath related to the earth, related to humanity, rather than tying it down to earth, weigh it down with earthly existence, as is the case by eating meat."[52]

However, Rudolf Steiner does not recommend a vegetarian diet to everyone, but only to spiritually striving people:

"This way of life is easily digestible, but whether everyone can do it for a long time, that's another question. Because a vegetarian life-style or vegetarianism without spiritual aspiration leads to illness. It is said that vegetarianism was known in Greece centuries before Christ and that the great sage of antiquity, Pythagoras, was the founder of vegetarianism. But here one must ask: Who was Pythagoras, and why did he live as a vegetarian?"[53]

---

52 GA 145 "Welche Bedeutung hat die okkulte Entwicklung des Menschen für seine Hüllen" (What Significance does the Occult Development of Man Have for his Sheaths), The Hague (Netherlands), lecture of March 21, 1913.

53 GA 266a "Aus den Inhalten der esoterischen Stunden" (From the contents of the esoteric lessons), Volume I, Appendix, internal lecture on nutrition and inner development. – In the esoteric lesson of August 13, 1908, in Stuttgart, Rudolf Steiner went into more detail: *"The vegetarian diet is excellent for doctors and lawyers, who are much more likely to see through their patients and their clients' business, but it is not right for bankers, industrialists, technicians, tradesmen, in short, for all that is connected with the work of calculation. For one loses by it the physical power of*

Now, in what way did the after-death and pre-birth existence in the Mars sphere find expression in the life of the author of this book?

Like many anthroposophists, he had already been connected with Christianity in two previous incarnations and had thus had the possibility to inwardly receive the Christ-impulse. [54] At the end of his last incarnation, the author died in the 16th century.[55] After living in the soul world, he reached the spiritual Mars sphere towards the end of the century. This was the time when the significant events described above took place. On all deceased Buddhists as well as all human souls that carried the Christ-impulse in their hearts and who at the time were going through their after-death development in the Mars sphere with awake consciousness, the Buddha's deed of salvation in 1604 and the accompanying effect on the culture of Mars made an extraordinarily deep impression. Therefore, they understandably developed a great reverence for the Buddha.

---

combination. That is why vegetarianism should never be praised so generally as it is often done in the world. It is also possible that one has got such a body by heredity, which cannot bear vegetarianism at all. Then one should simply not aspire towards esoteric training."

54 According to Rudolf Steiner, within the Anthroposophical Society there are essentially two groups of people who found their way to Christianity at different times and in different ways in their previous incarnations. Some felt attracted above all by the "cosmic Christianity" as well as the "anthroposophical cosmology", others more by the "abstract religious" of earthly Christianity and by the "Christian character" of Anthroposophy. See the lectures of July 8, 1924 in Dornach (GA 237, Volume 3 of "Karmic Relationships") and of July 18, 1924 in Arnhem/Netherlands (GA 240, Volume 4 of the same series). To which of the two groups the author belongs is evident from the subject of the present book as well as from the subjects of his previously published books.

55 In which way the author acquired knowledge of his previous incarnation will be described in a later chapter.

In case of the author this found its expression in an increasing interest for meditation already in the third seven-year period of his present earth life. One day towards the end of this period, seemingly by chance he came across the book "Die Lehre des Buddho[56] – Die Religion der Vernunft und der Meditation" (English edition: "The Doctrine of Buddha – The Religion of Reason") on a book table in front of a bookstore. With the greatest attention he immersed himself in the book and, from then on, he wanted to become a Buddhist.

Very soon he joined the Altbuddhistische Gemeinde, a German Community of Theravāda Buddhism[57], founded by Georg Grimm, the author of the above book in the Bavarian municipality of Utting am Ammersee (on the Lake Ammer). Immediately he travelled there and stayed for several days. Without having any prior knowledge about the division of life on earth into seven-year periods, this happened a few days before his 21st birthday, i.e. right at the beginning of his 4th seven-year period, in which the prenatal experiences of the Mars sphere are mirrored. Thus, during the first three years of his new seven-year period he was now a Buddhist steeped into the historically transmitted Buddha teachings of the Pali Canon. Therefore, he was able to absorb what one can still learn from Buddha today on earth.

This also was the time when, like many Western Buddhists, he felt a great devotion to Francis of Assisi. He even considered for a while

---

56 Author: Georg Grimm (1868 – 1945), founder of the "Altbuddhistische Gemeinde" in Germany, which was dissolved in 2002. In his books he mainly used the Pali term "Buddho" instead of the Sanskrit term "Buddha", because Buddha's teachings were at first written down in the Middle Indo-Aryan language Pali and collected in the so-called Pali Canon. These are the oldest Buddhist scriptures available to us today.

57 Theravada or "Doctrine of the Elders", is the name of the oldest existing school of Buddhism, in contrast to Mahāyāna (Great way) and Vajrayāna (Diamand way or Tibetan Buddhism).

whether he should become a Franciscan. This possibility arose because membership in the Altbuddhistische Gemeinde did not require one to leave the Christian church. However, his critical attitude towards the church, which had developed early in his youth due to the experiences mentioned before, stood in the way of joining the Franciscans. But perhaps it was no coincidence, that as a child he attended a kindergarten run by nuns of the "Regulated Third Order of St. Francis of Assisi". [58]

However, it is neither in the interest of Buddha nor of Christian Rosenkreutz, if people who have already gone through Christian incarnations want to become Buddhists or Franciscans on Earth. In the future, this should only happen during our stay in the Mars sphere. Fate had it that during another visit to Utting the author's attention was drawn to Rudolf Steiner's writings by a Buddhist. Already in the first books he read, he found references to Christian Rosenkreutz and the Rosicrucian path of education. This touched him very deeply and from then on he was increasingly drawn to Rosicrucianism.

No sooner he set out on this path a feeling overcame him that he had been led from Buddha via Rudolf Steiner to Christian Rosenkreutz. To his surprise, he found this feeling confirmed when, in one of Rudolf Steiner's lectures, he came across the statement already quoted above, according to which *"the most intimate disciple and friend of Christian Rosenkreutz was Gautama Buddha, living in the spirit body"*, who was sent by him to Mars, and that *"since the seventeenth century every human being, while within the Mars sphere, is for a time a Buddhist, a Franciscan, a direct follower of Francis of Assisi."* It appeared as if his experiences on earth were intimately connected with those events in

---

[58] See page 57.

the Mars sphere. Importantly, they clarified some of the pivotal experiences of his 4th seven-year period.

In the wake of these events, the author aspired to get closer to Christian Rosenkreutz by way of the Anthroposophical Society. But in the annual program at the local branch at that time he couldn't found anything about him, neither about the esoteric Christianity. So, he searched elsewhere and finally came to the Deutsche Rosenkreuzer-Gemeinschaft[59]. Their teachings bore a striking resemblance to anthroposophy. Therefore, he continued to read Rudolf Steiner's lectures with the greatest interest.

Unfortunately, he did not find any reference to the connection between the 4th seven-year period and the Mars sphere, which he had experienced so strongly. It wasn't until he reached the age of fifty plus that the fate guided him in Rudolf Steiner's comprehensive lecture opus to the statement where Steiner connects the 3rd seven-year period with the Sun sphere, and the 6th seven-year period with the Saturn sphere. Because of the fixed order of the planets, according to which the Sun sphere is followed by the Mars sphere, this suggested a connection of the latter with the 4th seven-year period, as well as of the Jupiter sphere with the 5th seven-year period.[60]

---

59 Former German section of *The Rosicrucian Fellowship*, founded in California by the Danish-born Carl Louis Frederik Grasshoff under the pseudonym Max Heindel. As it turned out later, Grasshoff had collected transcripts of lectures by Rudolf Steiner, translated them into English and published them as alleged revelations to him by an "Elder Brother" or Master of the Rosicrucians under the title "The Rosicrucian Cosmo-Conception", in German translation "Die Weltanschauung der Rosenkreuzer". See Rudolf Steiner's mention of this incident in GA 174b "Die geistigen Hintergründe des 1. Weltkrieges" (The Spiritual Background of World War I), Stuttgart, lecture of May 11, 1917.

60 See quote on page 33.

Between the last death of the author in the 16th century and his next birth in the 20th century there are only a few centuries. This may appear to some readers as an unbelievably short period of time for the existence in the higher worlds between two incarnations. Here, however, a peculiarity must be taken into account, of which Rudolf Steiner lets Maria speak to Ahriman in his mystery drama "The Soul's Probation", at the end of the 11th scene:

> *"In earthly evolution there are times*
> *In which the ancient forces slowly die,*
> *And dying, see the growth of newer ones.*
>
> *[...]*
>
> *In earth days of such kind, then seeds*
> *Are carefully planted into human souls,*
> *Which need a long time for full ripening.*
> *And people, in their next life, still must show*
> *Characteristics from their previous one.*
> *At such times, many men will be reborn*
> *As men in their succeeding life;*
> *And many women will be women again.*
> *The interval between the lives*
> *Is also shorter then than otherwise."*[61]

---

[61] German original wording by Rudolf Steiner: *"Es gibt im Erdenwerden solche Zeiten, in welchen alte Kräfte langsam sterben und sterbend schon die neuen wachsen sehn. [...] In solchen Erdentagen werden Keime in Menschenseelen sorgsam eingepflanzt, die lange Zeit zur vollen Reife brauchen. Die Menschen müssen dann im nächsten Leben noch Eigenschaften aus dem frühern zeigen. Es werden viele Männer solcher Zeiten in einem nächsten Leben wieder Männer; und viele Frauen werden Frauen wieder. Es ist dann auch die Zeitenlänge kürzer als jene, die sonst zwischen Leben liegt."*

In the same sense Rudolf Steiner expressed himself a decade later in one of his lectures in Oslo (formerly Kristiania):

"You all know that, normally, the period between death and rebirth is lengthy. But especially in the present phase of evolution, there are many human beings whose life between their last death and their present birth was only short." [62]

With the after-death transition from the Sun sphere to the Mars sphere, the spiritual world is revealed to us. In it, a completely new world of sound is added to the visionary, pictorial perceptions of the soul world. Powerful tones resound towards us in the Mars sphere from the spiritual environment. As in an orchestra, they complement each other to a great harmony of sound, which increases in intensity. In the ancient mystery schools, they were known as the "harmony of the spheres". This experience in the spiritual world can express itself in the earthly course of human life as an inclination towards music, especially classical music. The great composers such as Handel, Bach, Beethoven, Wagner, etc. received the inspirations for their wonderful orchestral works from their existence in the spiritual world. If the stay in the Mars sphere has made a strong impression on a person, love especially for classical music sometimes awakens in the youth and can then radiate throughout ones entire life on earth. With many, however, an intensification in this direction becomes apparent only with adolescence, when the spiritual individuality attains its independence, because only then does the influence of the Mars sphere, as the first region of the sounding spiritual world, make itself more strongly felt.

---

62 GA 209 "Nordische und mitteleuropäische Geistesimpulse" (Nordic and Central European Spiritual Impulses), Kristiania (Oslo, Norway), lecture of November 27, 1921.

The 5th Seven-Year Period and the Jupiter Sphere (Age: 28 – 35 Years)

The Mars sphere contains, as already mentioned, the spiritual archetypes of physical, inanimate things. Therefore, the deceased are still connected to the physical world there, even if only in a weak way. We finally detach ourselves from our last life on earth only with the transition from the Mars sphere to the Jupiter sphere.

"In the Jupiter sphere, the connection with the earth, so to speak, which up until now still continued slightly, becomes quite meaningless to the human being. " [63]

This makes it possible that in the 5th seven-year period of life on earth, which receives its imprint from the prenatal experiences in the Jupiter sphere, we look with some detachment at the sensations triggered by the sense world and consider them more rationally. This is the time when we develop the intellectual and feeling soul. We have become more thoughtful and reflective. In a way, this is an after-effect of the changed sound experience in the spiritual world, which is more substantial and meaningful in the Jupiter sphere than in the Mars sphere.

"It is not easy to characterize this life, this change of the harmony of the spheres. As it cannot be expressed in earthly words, we may use an analogy. The harmony of the spheres changes in the passage from Mars to Jupiter in such a way that can only be desribed as orchestral music to choral music. It becomes increasingly tone and that, which at the same time permeats the tone with meaning, expresses its actual being. The

[63] GA 140 "Okkulte Untersuchungen über das Leben zwischen Tod und neuer Geburt" (Occult Investigations on Life between Death and New Birth), Vienna (Austria), lecture of November 3, 1912.

harmony of the spheres receives content as we ascend into the sphere of Jupiter, and in the Saturn sphere full content is bestowed upon it as the expression of the Cosmic Word out of which everything has been created and which is found in the Gospel of St. John, «In the beginning was the Word.» This Word is the sounding-in of cosmic order and cosmic wisdom." [64]

In earthly life, this becomes noticeable in a temporarily stronger receptivity for church music or church hymns. Not only the inspirations for ecclesiastical hymns come from the Jupiter sphere, but also religious orchestral works such as Handel's "Hallelujah" or Wagner's overture to "Lohengrin". For as figure 12 on page 67 has shown, the Jupiter sphere and the Venus sphere interpenetrate each other. In both, religious experience plays a major role. In contrast to the Mars sphere, in which the spiritual archetypes of all inanimate physical things are to be found, in the Jupiter sphere we encounter the spiritual archetypes of all living things. Life as a universal, independent power already belongs to the realm of the supernatural, like everything divine and eternal as proclaimed by religions.

"In the next region [Jupiter sphere] the common life of the earthly world flows as thought being, as a fluid element, so to speak, of the «land of spirits». As long as one observes the world during physical embodiment, life appears to be confined within separate living beings. In the «land of spirits» it is liberated from them and, like life-blood, flows as it were through the whole land. It exists there as the living unity that is present in all things. Of this also only a reflection appears to man during earthly life, and this reflection expresses itself in every form of reverence that he pays to the whole, to the unity and harmony of the world. The religious life of man is derived from this reflection. He becomes aware of how far the all-embracing meaning of existence does not lie in what is

---

64 Ibidem.

transitory and separate. He regards the transitory as a similitude, a likeness of an Eternal, a harmonious unity. He looks up to this unity in a mood of reverence and worship. He performs before it religious rites and ceremonies." [65]

Because of the inner connection of the religious feeling with the life force, the former has a great influence on the development of the human etheric body, the supernatural bearer of life force in the human organism.

"A powerful means for the purification and ennoblement of the etheric body is religion. The religious impulses therefore have a great mission for the development of mankind." [66]

For many people who are not completely opposed to religion, it comes to the fore again in the 5th seven-year period of their life on earth. The external reason for this is often quite simply that they already have children of their own who are just passing through their 2nd seven-year period and are being accepted into a religious community. It is usually that of the parents. This brings back to them memories of their own childhood experiences. For many, this actually causes a kind of refreshment or deepening of their religious feeling. Some parents then take part in the church services again. Others, however, are already so critical of the church at this age that they remain members of their church community only formally or for the sake of the children.

---

[65] GA 9 "Theosophie" (Theosophy), section IV "Der Geist im Geisterland nach dem Tode" (The Spirit in the Land of Spirits after Death).

[66] GA 34 "Lucifer-Gnosis 1903 – 1908", essay "Die Erziehung des Kindes vom Gesichtspunkte der Geisteswissenschaft" (Education of the Child from the Point of View of Spiritual Science)

In their 5th seven-year period, many people therefore ask themselves whether it would not be more honest with themselves if they left the church. Most will probably remain with the church for the sake of their children, but there are also those who leave the church. The deeper reason for it lies in pre-birth experiences in the Jupiter sphere, which are mirrored in the 5th seven-year period of the earth life. While our after-death experiences in the Venus region are strongly dependent on whether and how closely we have connected into a religious denomination in the previous life, the forces from the Jupiter region, on the contrary, free us from it entirely.

"In the J u p i t e r r e g i o n, conditions which force the soul into some particular creed are dissolved. We have heard that the soul can pass through the Venus region with companionship only if it had adopted a creed; without religion it would be lonely and isolated there. We have also heard that the soul can pass through the Sun region properly only when it shows understanding for all the creeds. In the Jupiter region, however, the soul liberates itself entirely from the particular creed to which it belonged during life on Earth. This was not an essentially personal attachment but something into which it was born and was shared in company with other souls. Thus the soul can pass through the Venus region only if it has acquired religious ideas in earthly life; it can pass through the Sun region only if it shows understanding for all earthly beliefs. But the soul can pass through the Jupiter region only if it is able to liberate itself from the particular confession to which it belonged on Earth; merely to understand the others is not enough. For during the passage through the Jupiter region it will be decided whether in the next life the soul will have to be connected with the same creed as

before, or whether it has experienced everything that can be offered by one particular creed." [67]

In order to be able to assimilate these forces in the Jupiter region, the human being must be able to sustain a certain level of consciousness during his life after death until then. In our time, this is only possible if we have acquired a spiritual-scientific understanding of the spiritual foundations of all religions during our previous life on earth.

"In order that his consciousness shall not become dim, shall not fade away altogether after the Sun sphere, but that he can carry it over into the Mars sphere, into the Jupiter sphere, which he then has to pass through, it is necessary in the present cycle of human evolution that spiritual understanding of what is given in our religions and conceptions of the world shall take root in the human souls. Hence the endeavours to understand the essence of religions and systems of thought. Spiritual-scientific understanding will eventually be replaced by another, quite different understanding of which men today cannot even dream. For certain as it is that a truth is right in an epoch possessed of a genuine sense of truth, it is also a fact that continually new impulses will make their way into the evolution of humanity. True indeed it is that what Anthroposophy has to give is right for a particular epoch, and humanity, having assimilated Anthroposophy, may bear it into later times as assimilated impulses and through the assimilated forces also acquire the forces of the later epoch." [68]

In the author's earth life these influences from the Jupiter sphere expressed themselves during his 5th seven-year period in the way that he, as a member of a Rosicrucian Community, regularly held religious devotions in private, mostly together with other members. There was

---

67 GA 141 "Das Leben zwischen dem Tode und der neuen Geburt im Verhältnis zu den kosmischen Tatsachen" (Life between Death and new Birth in Relation to the Cosmic Facts), Berlin, lecture of 1 April 1913.

68 Ibidem, Berlin, lecture of November 20, 1912.

a whole series of different so-called "services", both for Sundays and for certain days of the week. This all reminded him very much of the Sunday and of the student church services, which he attended regularly from his second seven-year period on and, like all his classmates, even had to have his attendance confirmed in writing.

In the meantime, he had distanced himself more from the Catholic church. His understanding of Christ as a cosmic Sun spirit, and the conviction of reincarnation and karma had taken root in him to such an extent that his membership in the Catholic church, which strictly rejects these, had become a moral dilemma. Therefore, he would have liked to resign from the church right at the beginning of the 5th seven-year period. However, he was aware that such a step would have deeply upset his mother as well as his grandmother, who were both devout Catholics. He just could not do that to them. So, at first, he exited from the church inwardly. This was followed by an outer departure, however, not before the end of his 5th seven-year period at the age of 35, after both his grandmother and his mother had died. With that, a huge issue which had burdened him throughout the entire seven-year period, came to an end.

This account of the author's life should in no way be understood as a recommendation or even an invitation to resign from the church. As is well known, Rudolf Steiner, who was subject to rather severe hostilities on the part of the Catholic Church, did not resign. Nor did he advise others to do so, on the grounds that, according to church law at that time, resignation was not possible on account of the dogma of the infallibility of the pope. [69] On the other hand, in a lecture to the circle of

---

[69] *"The reason I do not advise Catholics to resign is because they have no right to resign under the present ecclesiastical constitution. In all seriousness. The Catholic has no right to resign from the Church, because by the dogma of infallibility such a decision has been made ex cathedra that the Catholic*

prospective priests of the Christian Community, Rudolf Steiner specifically described this dogma of infallibility as *"eminently anti-Christian".*[70]

In recent years, the number of people resigning from the church for a variety of reasons has rapidly increased. Ultimately, each individual must decide for himself or herself, after a thorough examination of conscience, whether or not to remain a member of his or her church. The final decision will only be made by higher powers during life after death in the Jupiter sphere.

At the time of the Graeco-Roman cultural epoch the Jupiter sphere had a stronger effect on earthly life, because until the end of their 5th seven-year period, up to the age of 35, people attained their soul-spiritual maturity in an entirely natural way. Therefore, the Romans worshipped Jupiter as their main deity. The Greeks called him Zeus.

---

cannot resign from the Church; he is simply still part of it, even if he himself declares that he is resigning." GA 342 "Vorträge und Kurse über christlich-religiöses Wirken – Teil I" (Lectures and Courses on Christian Religious Work – Part I), Stuttgart, discussion of June 15, 1912.

70 *"You know [...], in a certain moment was fixed the dogma of the so-called infallibility. This dogma of infallibility is accepted – this is the important thing –, adopted by many people. The one who is a real Christian can consider: What about this dogma of infallibility? – He can ask himself the question, for example: What would the first Fathers of the Church, who were still closer to the original sense of Christianity, have said about the dogma of infallibility? – They would have called it a blasphemy! And with this one would probably hit the mark in the Christian sense. But with it one would have pointed to an extraordinarily effective occult means, namely to awaken faith by something in the most eminent sense anti-Christian. But this faith is an important occult impulse towards a certain side, in order to get away from the normal Christian development."* (GA 174 "Zeitgeschichtliche Betrachtungen – Das Karma der Unwahrhaftigkeit – Teil 2" (Contemporary Historical Reflections – The Karma of Untruthfulness – Part 2), Dornach, lecture of January 22, 1917).

Jupiter was regarded as the ruler of the earth's atmosphere and its light phenomena, which reveal the beauty of earthly nature. In the seasonal changes of the earth they perceived the rhythm of all life. This was something profoundly sacred to them, because they feared death. As the ancient instinctive clairvoyance had faded away, they were left only with gloomy, frightening, shadowy perceptions.

In their religious feelings, the Greeks and Romans therefore turned not only to Zeus or Jupiter but also to the goddess Demeter (Roman: Ceres), who ruled over the earthly life processes. In autumn and winter, the withering and stagnation of nature was to them an expression of her mourning over the loss of her daughter Persephone (Roman: Proserpina). In spring and summer they experienced the blossoming and fruiting life as an expression of the goddess' joy of being allowed to be together with her daughter again, after her return from the dark realm of the dead. In Eleusis and other places of worship, mystery plays were performed, which brought this connection vividly to the consciousness of the audience. The Artemis cult at Ephesus was also dedicated to the worship of the divine life force, as shown by the symbols of fertility on the stone statue of the goddess that has survived to the present day.

The 6th Seven-Year Period and the Saturn Sphere (Age: 35 – 42 Years)

As already explained, when man has expanded to the Mars sphere in his life after death and has preserved a sufficient degree of consciousness, he experiences the spiritual archetypes of all inanimate, purely material things of the physical world. This includes his own former physical body. In the next higher Jupiter sphere the spiritual archetype of all life becomes additionally perceptible to him, which underlies his etheric or vital body as the carrier of life forces. As the deceased ascends in a further phase of development to the sphere of Saturn, he encounters the spiritual archetypes of everything related to soul life.

"The third region of «land of spirits» contains the archetypes of the soul world. All that lives in this world is here present as living thought being. We find in it the archetypes of desires, wishes and feelings, but here in the world of spirits nothing self-seeking clings to the soul. Just as all life forms a unity in the second region, so in this third region all longings, wishes, all likes and dislikes form a unity. The desire and wish of others are not separable from my desire and wish. The sensations and feelings of all beings are a common world, enclosing and surrounding everything else, just as the physical mantle of air surrounds the earth. This region is, as it were, the atmosphere of the «land of spirits»." [71]

This shows the inner relationship of the Saturn sphere with the Sun sphere, the highest region of the soul world. Both interpenetrate each other, as shown in Figure 12 (page 67), and have to do specifically with the "soul life" of human beings. Rudolf Steiner pointed out the connection of the Sun sphere with the 3rd seven-year period (age 14 - 21 years) and of the Saturn sphere with the 6th seven-year period (age 35 - 42 years):

"And in this way also human life must be considered. So, if an ill person between the a g e s o f f o u r t e e n a n d t w e n t y - o n e – this is an approximation – sought help from a physician in the mysteries, the physician knew: there are a number of diseases which simply have something to do with the passage of the person through the S u n s p h e r e on his descent from the planetary world into the physical

[71] GA 9 "Theosophie" (Theosophy), chapter "Der Geist im Geisterland nach dem Tode" (The Spirit in the Land of Spirits after Death).

world. If the patient was between thirty-five and forty-two, the mystery priest knew which diseases had something to do with the person's passage through the Saturn sphere on his descent. So, the physician foremost considered the connection of the life on earth with the experiences of a person in the existence between death and new birth." [72]

In the third seven-year period, when the forces of the Sun sphere are mirrored in our life on earth, we struggle to get a grip on the emotional surges in our astral body that accompany puberty. Three periods later, when we enter our sixth seven-year period at the age of 35, we pass through the higher, corresponding stage. Our life of soul has to contend with a new task. And in a similar way as puberty often begins three years before the age of 14, the emotional instability of middle age also becomes noticeable in many people three years before the age of 35. Psychologists call it the "midlife crisis". It can last up to three years beyond the end of the 6th seven-year period, that is until the age of 45.

At this age, many people check whether they are happy, or at the very least satisfied, with the hitherto course of their private and professional lives, whether they want to continue in the same way, or whether in the second half of their professional life that is about to begin, they want to devote themselves to another activity, which they have not been able to exercise so far, but which lives in their souls only as a an unrequited wish. As in the days of youth, the ideals and desires associated with our individuality resurface once more. Many people in their mid-thirties are now concerned with the question of whether their actions are really in harmony with their inner

---

[72] GA 218 "Geistige Zusammenhänge in der Gestaltung des menschlichen Organismus" (Spiritual Connections in the Formation of the Human Organism), Berlin, lecture of December 7, 1922.

convictions. Conscious activity, in accord with one's own ideals, is an expression of the development of the consciousness soul, which is the most spiritual member of the soul and is intimately connected with the "I".

By dint of our actions on earth we can develop a kinship with the Saturn sphere, so that we can live through it consciously after death. There, not only is it important whether one developed a genuine compassion in the preceding life on earth, which does not stop at national, cultural or religious borders, as it was a matter of importance already in the Sun sphere, but also whether we have acted in accordance with it. Our conscious and purposefully directed deeds are of decisive importance here.

"All that a person has carried out in his life on earth in the service of the community, in selfless devotion to his fellowmen, will bear fruit here because through this service, through this devotion, he has lived in a reflection of the third region of the «land of spirits». The great benefactors of the human race, the devoted natures, those who render great services to communities, have gained their ability to render them in this region after having acquired for themselves the entitlement to a special relationship to it during their previous earthly careers." [73]

Even when short of becoming one of the great benefactors of humanity, one can carry from the Saturn sphere into the next earth life the inclination of wanting to help other people. This can become noticeable especially in the 6th seven-year period, when our prenatal existence in the Saturn sphere is mirrored in life on earth.

In the case of the author this transpired in such a way that, from the age of 35 on, he began to feel a stronge urge to put the acquired

---

[73] GA 9 "Theosophie" (Theosophy), chapter "Der Geist im Geisterland nach dem Tode" (The Spirit in the Land of Spirits after Death).

spiritual teachings and ideals into concrete action rather than living with them only theoretically. Helping people in some way or another became his next goal. After a prolonged struggle with the new inner impulse, he decided in the middle of the seven-year period to train as a naturopath alongside with his former job. In his youth already he had collected medicinal herbs and was interested in alternative healing methods, and now the moment had evidently arrived to put this into practice. Towards the end of the seven-year period, three months before his 42nd birthday, he was finally awarded the official licence to practice naturopathy. It was time to change the profession.

Needless to say there are numerous ways of serving and helping other people, and the forces from the Saturn sphere can find their expression in diverse ways according to the each individual's interests and talents. But we always owe it precisely to the forces from this sphere that our spiritual ideals in us need not remain mere theory, but that we can translate them into real earthly deeds and act in accordance with the spirit.

But in another respect our after-death passage through the Saturn sphere, where we meet the archetypes of all that belongs to the soul, is of special importance especially for students of the spirit. It is there that we acquire the ability to form our corporeality in the next life on earth in such a way that it can become the bearer of a soul which is inclined to spirituality from childhood.

"If a person, let us say, has made an effort to concern himself with spiritual-scientific concepts in the present life on earth, then the passage through the Saturn sphere is actually particularly significant for his next life; for in this sphere the conditions are created so that a person can convert the forces which he acquires here through the knowledge of spiritual science or Anthroposophy into such forces which then plastically shape his corporeality, so that in his next life he then carries

within himself a kind of natural disposition to incline towards the spiritual already through his disposition. So, it can happen that a man grows up; he has been brought up as a materialist or as a Protestant or as a Catholic. He encounters Spiritual science and is receptive to it, does not reject it for this or that reason. Then he has absorbed it inwardly in his soul. Now he passes through the gate of death and once more traverses the Saturn sphere. There he absorbs forces which will predispose him in his next life to be the born spiritual person, and will, even as a child, demonstrate an inclination to the spiritual." [74]

In ancient Egyptian culture, this was still the case for most people, since they were maturing naturally until the age of 35 to 42 and were therefore very fond of everything spiritual.[75] While the Greeks and Romans only valued the light-filled above-ground world of the living and worshipped intensely their ruler Zeus or Jupiter as well as the regent of Life, Demeter or Ceres, the ancient Egyptians still maintained a more comprehensive world view. They matured naturally unto the 6th seven-year period, in which the influence of the Saturn sphere with the spiritual archetypes of everything concerning the soul comes to bear. Therefore, they were filled with a deep conviction that the human soul continues to exist after death in the soul-spiritual world. For the Egytians the realm of the dead had not yet become the shadowy realm of the Greeks, dark as the earthly world in a moonless night and ruled by a bleak, foreboding god like the Roman Saturn, the Greek Hades or Pluton.

At the beginning of their cultural epoch, the realm of the dead was for ancient Egyptians still a world which they experienced as

---

[74] GA 140 "Okkulte Untersuchungen über das Leben zwischen Tod und neuer Geburt" (Occult Investigations on Life between Death and New Birth), Munich, lecture of March 12, 1913.

[75] Cf. page 70/71.

illuminated by the light of the brightly shining full moon, ruled by the wise god Osiris. Thus, they worshipped him and his sister and wife Isis in accord with the phases of the moon.[76]

Isis was recognized as the regent of the soul. She widened the noble parts of the human individual souls after death to an all-encompassing soul in correspondence to an after-death life in the Saturn sphere. In doing so, the possibility was given to the deceased of uniting with the Osiris, to become Osiris themselves. At that time people "died towards Osiris", in a sense of the modern Rosicrucian dictum: "In Christo morimur - into Christ or in Christ we die". This was already prepared in the ancient Egyptian cult of Isis and Osiris.

The 7th Seven-Year Period and the Sphere of the Zodiac (Age: 42 - 49 Years)

At the age of 42 to 49 the influences from the 4th region of the spiritual world express themselves in the earthly course of life. It contains the spiritual archetypes of everything that man alone only contributes to the earthly external world through creative activity.

"It is, however, through him that there are in the world all the creations of the arts, sciences, engineering, states and governments et cetera — in short, all that he has embodied in the world as original creations of his spirit. Without his activity, no physical expressions of all this would exist in the world. The archetypes of these purely human creations are in the fourth region of the «land of spirits». All that humans develop during earthly life in the way of scientific discoveries, of

---

[76] See, e.g., GA 106 "Ägyptische Mythen und Mysterien" (Egyptian Myths and Mysteries), Leipzig, lecture of September 8, 1908.

artistic ideas and forms, of technical conceptions, bears fruit in this fourth region. It is out of this region therefore that artists, scientists and great inventors draw their impulses and enhance their genius during their stay in the «land of spirits» in order, during another incarnation, to be able to assist in fuller measure the further evolution of human culture. But we must not imagine that this fourth region of the «land of spirits» possesses importance only for specially outstanding human beings. It has great importance for all human beings. All that occupies man in physical life outside the sphere of everyday living, wishing and willing has its source in this region. If man did not pass through it in the period between death and rebirth, he would in his subsequent life have no interests leading out beyond the narrow circle of our personal life-conduct to the general-human."[77]

However, what people experience here and how much they are able to absorb in terms of forces depends entirely on their stage of development in the previous life on earth.

"They can enjoy in the «land of spirits» only the fruits of what it was possible for them to carry out in accordance with their talents and the degree of development of the folk and state et cetera into which they were born."

During the current epoch humans can create in the outer physical world only what is lifeless and soulless, and only the physical objects exert an effect on the senses which ignites the I-consciousness. This indicates an inner connection of the 4th region of the spiritual world both with the Mercury sphere as well as the Mars sphere.

The Mercury sphere is the first region of the higher soul world. Its forces give the 1st seven-year period of human life on earth its character. It serves above all the development of the physical body and

[77] GA 9 "Theosophie" (Theosophy), chapter "Der Geist im Geisterland nach dem Tode" (The Spirit in the Land of Spirits after Death).

the initial awakening of the I-consciousness through the physical sense organs.

The Mars sphere is the first region of the spiritual world. Its forces are mirrored in the 4th seven-year period of earthly life, in which the bearer of our I becomes available to us.

In the 7th seven-year period, which extends over the age of 42 to 49 years, not the I-bearer, but the I itself, the first spiritual member of our being, is freed up for further development. This happens under the influence of the forces of a sphere which no longer belongs to the planetary spheres, but is the lowest region of the fixed stars. It contains the twelve forces of the zodiac, which give rise both to the twelve physical senses of the earthly human body and to the upright human posture as shown in Figure 5 (page 20) in connection with the signs of the zodiac. Both of these are essential physical prerequisites for the attainment of our I-consciousness in the earthly domain.

The development of our I as an independent spiritual member requires that we detach ourselves from the group soul of which we were previously a part of. The people of antiquity still felt very strongly as members of their people or tribe. Even today, there are many who still feel that way. Others may no longer feel strongly bound ethnically or nationally, but still identify to a great extent with the circle of family and kinfolk. Ultimately, however, each person must eventually separate from these blood connections in order to be able to become a free, independent I.

So as not to succumb to egotism on this path of development towards the free individuality, one is called upon to develop a general-human interest and compassion which recognizes and values all other humans as "I"s of equal worth. In this way, kinship by blood will be replaced by kinship of the spirit. We will then feel ourselves as a community of cosmic spirit beings with equal rights, who from time to time incarnate in earthly bodies.

To make this development possible, the cosmic being of Christ descended to earth and united himself with humanity through the Mystery of Golgotha. He is the great leader of the human I-development, which is so intimately connected with the forces of the zodiac. This was demonstrated figuratively to his contemporaries on earth by surrounding himself with the twelve apostles. He appeared as the thirteenth in their midst, like the sun in the sky surrounded by the twelve forces of the zodiac.

"Then, something new entered the earthly spiritual atmosphere. Whoever does not admit that something else is now spiritually present on earth than was there thousands of years ago, does not understand Christianity and its preparation. Only those who look at it in this way, that something real and actual came as a new impact, know what happened there at the beginning of Christianity. If you look at it in this way, you will also find the expression for the transformation of the earth planet in the Spiritual and will have to say to yourself: All closer blood ties are breaking. Everything that has held people together in small communities based on the blood is gradually breaking. The small fraternal unions are gradually being extended to the great fraternal union which is to embrace all people on earth, where every person says brother to every person, where man «leaves mother and father and brother and sister». Everything, which blood had brought about as a kind of group-'I', an I that goes beyond the ordinary I, has to disappear from the earth. [...]

Christ Jesus was the one, who set himself the task to give the impulse, the power to establish this fraternal union. Therefore, the mission of the Christ Jesus and the ideal of Christianity is expressed in the words: «Whoever does not leave father, mother, brother and sister cannot be my disciple.» Hence also the rejection, «This is not my mother. My mother and my brothers are those who do the will of my Father.» [78] *This is the new spirit that is to come into humanity in contrast to the blood."* [79]

This sublime influence flows to us especially from the fourth region of the spiritual world, the sphere of the zodiac, which contains the forces that form the I, which make us truly individual human beings. In the 7th seven-year period of life on earth, at the age of 42 to 49, this is expressed in the fact that many people are confronted with tasks and situations in which they are completely or at least very much on their own. In the process of coping with these tasks or circumstances, the I develops a stronger independence. This, of course, does not necessarily call for separating from the family and going one's own way. We must not abandon other people. Even within the family ties, for example, in the parental role, we can find ourselves confronted with situations in which we are challenged to develop independence and be able to hold our own.

Looking at the seven-year periods in general, we find that during the first three years the physical-material tasks predominate. During the third to fifth years of each seven-year period, aspects of the soul development stand in the foreground, whereas the fifth to seventh years are invariably related to the development of the preliminary stages of the higher spiritual members of our being. The I, as the lowest spiritual member of being, is particularly related to the fourth and to the middle year of each seven-year period. Figure 13 offers a schematic overview. For the sake of clarity, the illustration omits the fact that each member overlaps half the way with the preceding as well as with the following one, just as each cosmic sphere has an effect

---

[78] Matthew 12:48-50

[79] GA 96 "Ursprungsimpulse der Geisteswissenschaft" (Original Impulses of Spiritual Science), Berlin, lecture of March 25, 1907.

on the upper half of the preceding and the lower half of the following one.

Thus, Rudolf Steiner's statement about the earliest I-experience of the human being becomes understandable: *"The child only really learns to live in the I, to know about the I, after about the third year."* [80]

With the third year the soul development of the child intensifies and in the fourth year the soul finds its center in the I. But because the soul is intimately connected with the astral body, as is the physical body with the etheric body, a first, temporary glimmer of the I-consciousness is possible in exceptional cases already from the second birthday, i.e., at the beginning of the third year of life. By then the development of the astral body and the sentient soul, both of which are connected with the I, already intensifies.

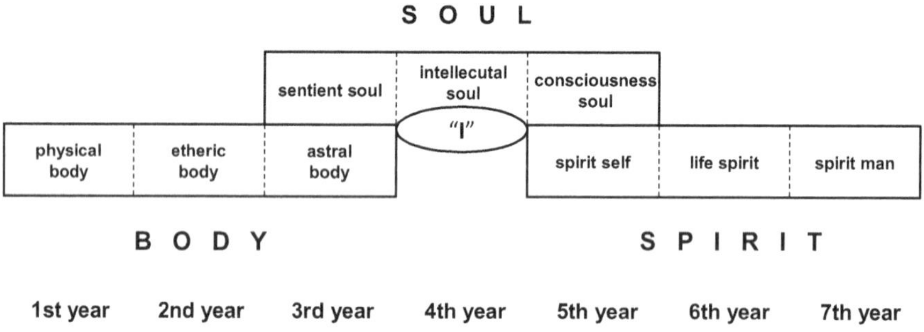

Figure 13:
The relationship of the members of the human being to the individual years of each 7-year period

[80] GA 127 "Die Mission der neuen Geistesoffenbarung" (The Mission of the New Revelation of the Spirit), Zürich (Switzerland), lecture of February 25, 1911.

Let us turn back and consider the 7th seven-year period and its connection with the zodiac and the strengthening of the I. How does this express itself in the life on earth. An example from the life of the author may help to illustrate this.

Towards the end of his 6th seven-year period, his father had died, exactly seven years after the death of his mother. Thus, he was without parents from the 7th seven-year period. At the same time, he changed his occupation which led him to become self-employed as naturopath. He moved from the south to the centre of Germany to take over a medical practice. A series of external events led to the fact that the move took place just two days before his 42nd birthday and thus exactly at the beginning of his new seven-year period, although he had not intended it that way.

On account of the now greater distance to his former circle of friends, the contacts gradually loosened during the following years. There were no more work colleagues either. In addition, there was a separation in his private life, by mutual agreement, so that in the end he was completely severed from all previous connections and ended up entirely on his own. In the 4th year of the seven-year period he experienced this with particular intensity as a sort of duality between the "I" and the world. The world together with its beings now appeared to him as a singular opposite. It had now become his "you", like a macrocosmic I, according to which he was modelled as a microcosmic I.

This loneliness drove the author to seek refuge in the spirit. Thus, he turned inwardly to Christ as well as to Christian Rosenkreutz, looking for guidance and a clue how to continue the spiritual path. The clue was received before too long and led him to his joining the Anthroposophical Society. This happened in the 5th year of this seven-year period, which is related to the spirit-self, exactly 3 x 7 years after he joined the Rosicrucian Fellowship. At that time, also in the 5th year of the period, he felt guided by Buddha and Rudolf Steiner to Christian Rosenkreutz. This time he felt that he was led by Christian Rosenkreutz to Rudolf Steiner, exactly the opposite as during the 4th seven-year period. From now on he took to daily reading of Rudolf Steiner's lectures with even greater intensity then before and to extending his study of Anthroposophy to previously unread material.

The fact that the 7th seven-year period of the human life on earth is connected with the zodiac also results from a look back to the primeval Persian culture. The people of that time matured in a natural way until the age of 42 - 49 years[81] and were therefore particularly receptive for the influence of the zodiacal sphere from their 7th seven-year period, although they were not yet capable of full I-development. This began only two cultural epochs later, namely during the Greco-Latin culture. However, the founder of the primeval Persian culture, the first Zarathustra, also called Zoroaster, was already able, due to the developmental stage of mankind, to enlighten his disciples about the great importance and the work of the highest sun-spirit Ahura Mazdao or Ormuzd. He could perceive Him as the great spiritual aura of the sun and taught his contemporaries that the work of Ahura Mazdao finds its pictorial expression in the sense world in the course of the sun through the signs of the zodiac, like a scriptural sign in the sky. The Latin word "zodiacus" has its origin in the primeval Persian culture:

"To them it was a most important sign that Ahura Mazdao, in order to accomplish his creations and manifestations in the world, should, in the language of Modern Astronomy, apparently 'describe a circle' in the celestial space. This describing of a circle was regarded as the expression

---

81 See page 70.

of a graphic character that Ahura Mazdao or Ormuzd makes known to the people, indicating in what manner he works and how he integrates his activities into the world as a whole. It is important that Zarathustra was able to point out that the Zodiac as a line returning to itself in space, is the expression of time returning to itself. There is indeed a most profound significance underlying the statement, that one branch of time leads to the future, forward, the other to the past, backward. Zaruana Akarana is what later became known as the Zodiac, that self-contained time-line described[82] *by Ormuzd, the Spirit of Light. This is the expression of the spiritual activity of Ormuzd. The passage of the sun across the zodiacal images is an expression of the activity of Ormuzd; while the Zodiac itself is the symbol of Zaruana Akarana. In reality, «Zaruana Akarana» and «Zodiacus» are identical terms, just in the same way as are «Ormuzd» and «Ahura Mazdao».*" [83]

"Time returning into itself" marks the state of eternity in the sphere of the zodiac. The phenomenon of time is a phenomenon of the soul world and it reaches into the spiritual world only as far as its spheres are penetrated by the spheres of the soul world. This influence reaches as far as the Saturn sphere, as Figure 12 (page 67) shows. The sphere of the zodiac lies above the temporal regions. As the fourth region of the spiritual world, the zodiac is no longer subject to the temporal influence of the soul world. Instead, in it already prevails the quality of timelessness or eternity, which is inherent in all spheres of the starry heavens. And since with our I we belong to the timeless region of the zodiac, we take part in eternity and hence are immortal spirit beings.

---

82 in the sense of "performed in the sky"

83 GA 60 "Antworten der Geisteswissenschaft auf die großen Fragen des Daseins" (Answers of Spiritual Science to the Great Questions of Existence), Berlin, lecture of January 19, 1911.

What we know today as astrology and astronomy has a common origin and stems from the primeval Persian culture. So it is by no means a coincidence that the three "magi" or "king-initiates from the East" mentioned in the Bible indeed came "from the East"[84], from that region where at the time remnants of the original star-lore of ancient Persia and the old, instinctive clairvoyance had been preserved among some tribes. Therefore, by observing changes in the starry sky, which conjured imaginations in their souls, it was possible for the initiates to obtain indications of the time and place of birth of the long-anticipated Jesus child.[85]

What survives to this day as astrology of the antiquity, are teachings, put down in writings only in a time when the primeval Persian star-wisdom of Zarathustra had long since become an externalized tradition and was greatly changed.

The 8th Seven-Year Period and the Sphere of the Spirit-Self (Age: 49 – 56 Years)

Beyond the sphere of the zodiac lies the fifth region of the spiritual world. It is at the same time the first level of the higher spiritual world, although, from a somewhat broader perspective, already the fourth region, the zodiacal sphere, can also be assumed to belong there.

---

84 Matthew 2.

85 Clemens Brentano (1778 - 1842), a German poet and novelist, reports in his book "Das Leben der heil. Jungfrau Maria" (The Life of the Holy Virgin Mary), what the stigmatized nun Anna Katharina Emmerick or Emmerich (1774 - 1824) told him from her visions about the star-lore practiced for centuries among the tribes of the holy three kings.

In the fifth region of the spiritual world the true self of the human being is at home, the "spirit-self". In his book "Theosophy", Rudolf Steiner describes it as follows:

"What he is here, is really he himself — the being who receives an external existence in the numerous and varied incarnations. In this region the true self of man can run free in all directions, and this self is thus the being who appears ever anew in each incarnation as the one. This self brings with it the faculties that have developed in the lower regions of the «land of spirits». It consequently carries the fruits of former lives over into those following. It is the bearer of the results of former incarnations."

Two pages after that Rudolf Steiner writes:

"Since man in the fifth region lives in his own true self, he is lifted out of everything from the lower worlds that envelops him during his incarnations. He is what he ever was and ever will be during the course of his incarnations. He lives in the governing power of the intentions that prevail during these incarnations, and that he grafts into his own self. He looks back on his own past and feels that all he has experienced in it will be integrated into the intentions he has to realize in the future. There flash forth a kind of remembrance of his earlier, and a prophetic vision of his future lives." [86]

As the human being during life after death expands into the starry world beyond the zodiac, he reaches the spheres which are the fount of the primal forces for all regions below. And just like near the top of the mountain one obtains a panoramic view of the landscape below, the first region of the higher spiritual world offers an overview of the

---

[86] GA 9 "Theosophie" (Theosophy), chapter "Der Geist im Geisterland nach dem Tode" (The Spirit in the Land of Spirits after death).

past incarnations to those human souls who are able to preserve there a degree of consciousness.

In ancient India, at the time of the primeval Indian culture of the 8th to 6th millennium B.C., people ascended to such an overview as a natural gift as soon as they reached the age of 49 to 56, the years of their 8th seven-year period.[87] Therefore, especially in the religions of India, both in Hinduism and in Buddhism, the teachings of reincarnation and karma have been preserved. However, over millennia, errors crept into these traditional teachings, as was the case with the star wisdom of the ancient Persians. Many distortions and falsehoods led to the doctrine of the so-called "transmigration of souls", according to which, depending on their karma, humans could incarnate as animals of different stages of development, and, similarly, animals could also return as humans.

This view probably came about because in the pre-Christian cultures of the East the I-consciousness was not yet very pronounced. The primeval Indians knew from inner experiences that they were spiritual beings and that they belonged to the spiritual world. However, they did not really feel themselves as individuals, but rather belonging to a group soul or a group spirit. Such is the case in the animal kingdom, where a group spirit differentiates into the bodies of animals. Thus, an individual animal does not have a permanent existence, but is absorbed again into the group spirit after its death. The consciousness of the primeval Indians was furthermore still strongly interspersed with dreams, similar to the dreamlike picture consciousness of the higher animals.

In contemporary culture, reaching the age of 49 to 56 and the connection with the sphere of the spirit-self is generally expressed in

---

[87] See page 70.

the mood of looking back at one's life so far. We are then beyond those seven-year periods in which our earthly body is built up by the forces of the planetary spheres and the zodiac. As a result, we go through the so-called menopause. In a female incarnation this is expressed in stronger hormonal changes than in a male incarnation. Certain biological processes gradually fade away. In both sexes, however, this phase is understandably associated with a certain emotional unrest and instability, because it is accompanied by changes in the astral body which are involved in the transformation of a part of it into the spirit-self. Spirit is the antipole of substance. Therefore, the spiritualization of the human being in the second half of life inevitably results in a decrease of the material processes that sustain the body.

At the beginning of his 8th seven-year period, in the 49th year of his life, the author also noticed how an inner drive to look back on the periods of his life on earth that he had already lived through began to stir. As a result, he carried out intensive memory work over the next three years. In order to be able to arrange the individual memories chronologically, he created a tabular "life plan", similar to a timetable used in school. Thus, for each year of his life on earth, he got an empty field in which he could write notes about the events of that year.

1st 7-year period	0	1	2	3	4	5	6
2nd 7-year period	7	8	9	10	11	12	13

Figure 14: Scheme of a table for creating a life plan

At first, he was only able to assign a precise time to the most important events. But from day to day, from week to week, the table filled up more and more, and he finally received a detailed overview of his entire life on earth up to that point. On this basis, he then repeatedly transported himself back to past experiences and tried to remember everything as vividly as possible and to experience it in inner living images as if it were the present. This is possible because all past experiences are stored in our etheric body. With some practice we can recall many of them and bring them to vivid inner imagination.

Such a purely mental activity is at the same time an occult exercise, because memories are of a supersensory nature. One can neither see them with physical eyes, nor hear them with ears, nor grasp them with hands. In this way, one also rises from the spatial experience in the present into a purely temporal experience of the past, which is related to that which we experience in the soul world after death. By consciously practicing this, we are active in the supernatural and thereby come into closer contact with our angel. Rudolf Steiner explained in this regard:

"And this brings me to a significant chapter of spiritual cognition. Suppose you are reflecting, in human self-knowledge, on memory, on the ability to remember. You say, I use my inner organ, my soul organ, for the ability to remember. – But if you look with full consciousness on what you are looking at then, you must look in such a way that you say to yourself: In this whole activity, in this process of remembering, the Angelos is weaving and living inside. – Try right now, at this moment, to remember something you experienced yesterday, any event. Then you have let an inner soul process taking place. In what is going on there, and in that a thought of yesterday arises in you, an experience of

yesterday manifests to you in the memory anew, inside there is an angel working."[88]

The Angeloi or angelic beings are those spiritual entities that guide us from earth life to earth life. They have already fully developed the spirit-self and were therefore appointed guardians of the human spirit-self as well. Therefore, every angel overlooks all incarnations of the human being guarded by him.

The author noticed, in the course of his memory work described above and the accompanying closer connection with his angel, how in him the desire became stronger and stronger to learn something about his previous incarnation. At that time he was not yet aware that in the 8th seven-year period, in which he was at the time, the prenatal experiences from the 5th region of the spiritual world, the sphere of the spirit-self, become effective in the soul, so that from this age on the conditions are particularly favourable to learn something about one's own previous incarnation or even earlier incarnations. At the same time he felt called upon to meditate even more in the following period in order to improve his receptivity for supersensory perceptions.

In the fourth year of his 8th seven-year period, which – like in every other seven-year period – is connected with the I of the human being, first inklings regarding his previous incarnation arose in him inwardly. However, he was clear about the fact that here extreme caution is of essence, because one can thereby entangle oneself all too easily in an illusion. Therefore, he accepted the inklings at first only as possibilities and left them quite consciously in the state of suspension. He was not able to gain clarity about them on his own. But the inklings grew stronger and increasingly pointed in a certain direction.

---

[88] GA 196 "Geistige und soziale Wandlungen in der Menschheitsentwicklung" (Spiritual and Social Transformations in Human Development), Dornach, lecture of February 13, 1920.

In the following fifth year, he finally turned to Christ and to his angel in prayer, saying: "If it is karmically possible and does not hinder my further development, I would like to know who I was in my former earthly life. But not my will, but Yours be done." With this prayer, he completely (!) surrendered his wish to his higher guidance and left everything else to God's will. He felt quite clearly that now he would just have to wait, because the spiritual world dispenses by grace, and only when it considers the gift to be justified. A few weeks later his wish was granted, quite in accordance with the following words of Rudolf Steiner, which the author discovered only later:

"We have to assign to each person one Being, who, being one stage higher than humans, can lead the individuality over from one incarnation to the other. [...] These are just watchful beings, who preserve the memory, so to speak, from one incarnation to the other, as long as the human being himself is not able to do so. These Beings are the Angeloi or Angels. Thus we can say, each man is a personality in each incarnation, and over each man a being watches, who has a consciousness which reaches from incarnation to incarnation. This makes it possible that in certain lower grades of initiation, man is able, even if he does not himself know anything about his past incarnations, to ask his Angel about them. This is quite possible for certain lower grades of initiation." [89]

Lower degrees of initiation can already be achieved by following the instructions Rudolf Steiner set out in his book "How to gain knowledge of the higher worlds". The procedure explained there is still today the safest way of entry into spirit discipleship. Meditation and concentration have an organizing effect on our astral body and

---

[89] GA 110 "Geistige Hierarchien und ihre Wiederspiegelung in der physischen Welt" (Spiritual Hierarchies and their Reflection in the Physical World), Düsseldorf, lecture of April 15, 1909.

make it receptive to the supersensory world. This enables our spiritual guidance to come into closer contact with us from within and to direct our further development in more targeted manner. However, inner perceptions can also lead completely astray. For this reason every communication from within, no matter whether it happens in the form of pictures or by words, requires a most thorough examination!

It is favourable here if the message coming from inside is supported by one coming at the same time from outside. This is what happened to the author. One day his inkling, which occurred with increasing frequency, was also confirmed from the outside, and that in a very special moment. On the very same day he also received an inner confirmation, in that ten memories were placed into his consciousness at once, all of which were related to his previous incarnation. This shows how important the memory work carried out by the author in the years before was, because now his angel could select the most important events from the rich treasure of memories and place them into his consciousness. In this way, he was made aware of how many things connected with his past incarnation run like a recurrent theme through his present life, without him ever having noticed it before.

Only later did the author find confirmation from Rudolf Steiner about his feeling that the confirmation coming from outside is particularly important. During a Berlin lecture of 1916, Rudolf Steiner spoke thus to his audience:

"If you are to know anything about your previous incarnation, in our era you will not understand it from within yourself. Rather, your attention will be drawn to it through some outer event or through another person. In our time, it is generally false when somebody looks

within and then claims to have been this or that person. If we are to know anything, it will be told to us from outside." [90]

Rudolf Steiner himself had also received such an external reference to his previous incarnation in the course of a conversation with the Cistercian Father Wilhelm Neumann in Vienna:

"And then a noteworthy episode occurred. I was once giving a lecture in Vienna. The same person was there and after the lecture he made a remark which could only be interpreted in the sense that at this moment he had complete understanding of a certain man belonging to the present age and of the relation of this man to his earlier incarnation. And what the person said on that occasion about the connection between two earthly lives, was correct, was not false. But through his intellect he understood nothing; it simply came from his lips." [91]

The words that were so significant for Rudolf Steiner were: *"The germs of this lecture you have given us today come from Thomas Aquinas!"* [92]

Rudolf Steiner received this hint already in his 4th seven-year period. We do not know whether he already broke through to his previous incarnation at that time. Should he have succeeded in doing so only in a later seven-year period, the experience reported by him certainly belongs to those events which have to do with the earlier incarnation and which run like a recurrent theme through our present one.

---

[90] GA 169 "Weltwesen und Ichheit" (World-Being and I-ness), Berlin, lecture of July 18, 1916.

[91] GA 240 "Esoterische Betrachtungen karmischer Zusammenhänge – Band VI" (Karmic Relationships – Vol. 6), Arnhem (Netherlands), lecture of July 18, 1924.

[92] GA 74 "Die Philosophie des Thomas von Aquino" (The Philosophy of Thomas Aquinas), Dornach, lecture of May 24, 1920.

Many people probably have experiences of a similar kind, but they often go by unnoticed or are misinterpreted. In connection with the question of a former incarnation, the help by an outer experience is a requirement in our time, even if someone has already reached such a high level of supersensory perception, as it was the case with Rudolf Steiner. In principle, it would be possible, through a certain development of the forces of speech, to obtain a direct view into earlier incarnations. But this would inevitably be connected with the fact that the person concerned would be subject to the worst possible temptations, for the forces of speech are connected with the sexual forces, as is evident by the change of voice in male adolescents. That is why the spiritual leadership of mankind today makes use of other means.

"One of these means may strike one as strange, but it rests upon a profound truth. Suppose that a person develops the inner life; it would need too much of an effort, and perhaps lead to too much temptation, were he to look back karmically at his former lives by developing the speech-forces. Therefore the spiritual beings have recourse to another means, which many suppose to be merely accidental. He may meet, for example, a person who mentions a name, or a certain time, or a certain people. This works externally upon his soul in such a way that as a result he may develop the necessary forces to serve as a support for clair-voyance etc., and he will then notice that this name or hint will lead to a retrospective view of his past lives, without any knowledge of this on the part of the speaker. This is a case of outer means being resorted to. The man in question hears a name or an era or a nation mentioned, and is thereby stimulated from outside, as it were, to look back into his former earthly incarnations. Such external stimuli are sometimes of great importance to a clairvoyant observation of the world. One has what seems to be an entirely accidental experience, but from this rays forth a

stimulus for clairvoyant forces which one otherwise would have developed only in rudimentary form." [93]

The author of the present book has by no means developed sufficient powers to allow a direct look into his former life. Nevertheless, he may consider the hint from outside, which came to him in a certain situation and in an unmistakable way, as an analogous experience to the process described here by Rudolf Steiner. Shortly thereafter also followed the above-mentioned conformation from within by way of the ten memories. During the following weeks and months further confirmations were added and up to the present day not a single event has transpired which would contradict.

Furthermore, it is interesting in this context that this revelation befell the author just at the age of 53, namely, in the fifth year of the seven-year period, which has to do in a very special way with the spirit-self that comprises our previous incarnations. [94]

When someone on the path of spirit discipleship reaches the point of having the above-mentioned experiences, one should be expressly made aware of the fact that they are always connected with trials. In case of the author this process began with the fact that he was requested first from within to write down all memories that were revealed to him in connection with his former incarnation because soon thereafter he would be subjected to an attempt from the side of Ahriman persuading him that it was all an illusion. Weeks later this announced trial actually took place. Now, with the help of his notes, he could recall all the details and thus resist the temptation. Here the

---

93 GA 140 "Okkulte Untersuchungen über das Leben zwischen Tod und neuer Geburt" (Occult Investigations on Life between Death and New Birth), Bergen (Norway), lecture of October 11, 1913.

94 See figure 13, page 104.

author found it extraordinarily helpful that by then he had already read Rudolf Steiner's Mystery Dramas several times. Specifically, he was thoroughly familiar with the 11th scene of "The Soul's Probation" where Maria refutes Ahriman's misleading assertion that the remembrance of her former life which she had just experienced was only a delusion.[95]

However, even before this Ahrimanic trial, the author had been subjected to one by Lucifer. Typically, such trials come from within. Several memories are brought vividly to one's consciousness, even of the kind that one has long forgotten, but which are to serve as proof of the connection with an alleged previous incarnation. Whoever has already developed occult hearing of some degree, or has perhaps already brought it with him into the present life as a natural gift which can certainly happen, will be able to observe that, after his angel or his spirit guide has spoken to him inwardly, the voice of the tempter can follow in the same "tone" and words, which cannot be distinguished in any way from the former. It will therefore make a great impression! The temptation can, for example, consist of being seduced to believe that one is a rather special individual, perhaps a historical personality, and thus a worthy cause of flattery.

In the case of the author, the Luciferic temptation happened in such a way that, shortly after the above-mentioned ten memories, three further, though completely different memories surfaced in his consciousness. One of them, which he had completely forgotten, suggested that he had been a certain person who lived on earth at the time of and in the immediate proximity of Christ Jesus. Of course, this made the matter appear very questionable to the author. Nevertheless, it lasted a few weeks until he succeeded, by thorough investigation, to

---

95 See page 84.

see through this deception, and thus to pass the test. After a prolonged and intensive search he could find neither reminiscences nor a recurrent theme in his memory store, which could have served as a proof that this alleged earlier incarnation has left traces in the present life. The lesson he learned was that he must never rely on the "sound" of the inner voice perceived by occult hearing, nor on an image conjured up by the inner vision.

Here, too, it was helpful that the author had previously deepened the study of the Mystery Dramas and was thus forewarned and prepared. No one can progress on the path of spirit discipleship without being subjected to such trials from time to time. They are an indispensable part on the path of inner development and ultimately further the process of maturation.

The mirroring of the sphere of the spirit-self in the 8th seven-year period had yet another, rather different effect for the author. When we have expanded to this sphere after death and have been able to preserve a certain degree of consciousness, we not only have an overview of our past incarnations, but also look from outside at the zodiac and at the planetary spheres contained within. This allowed the author a previously not attainable access to Rudolf Steiner's statements about the lemniscatory paths of the planets, which were not only difficult to understand but also seemingly contradictory. Of course, in the higher spiritual world we do not see physical stars or planetary bodies or orbits, but only spiritual entities and forces. However, the after-effect of such experience mirrored into the earthly life stimulated in the author to raise himself by a pictorial imagination beyond the zodiac and to reimagine it and the planets moving within by way of sense-free thinking. This made it possible for him to penetrate step by step those realizations and concepts, which he published in his book "The Lemniscatory Path System". Many of the illustrations contained therein were drawn from the above perspective.[96]

These are only two examples of how the mirroring of the sphere of the spirit-self can have an effect in the 8th seven-year period of life on earth. Of course, a great many variations on the theme will appear here, depending on the degree of consciousness which an individual had in this sphere in life after death. For example, it happens that some people in their 8th seven-year period begin to be interested in the Middle Ages, or their attention is drawn to this time by some external occurrences, because many of us had a former incarnation during this period. It may be that someone begins to read historical novels or biographies of persons of the Middle Ages or finds pleasure in visiting medieval buildings, perhaps even entering a cathedral where he or she has been in the previous incarnation. The fact that there are so many medieval clubs and markets today could be a sign that people are gradually beginning to remember their previous incarnations, even if at first only emotionally and rather subconsciously.

Furthermore, there are cases in which the after-death review of the past life plays less of a role than the pre-birth experience in the sphere of the spirit-self or in the 5th region of the spiritual world at the descent into the present earth life. After we have passed through the middle between two incarnations, dreaming or even sleeping, we become more awake again and henceforth turn our attention to the earth. We begin to influence our ancestral lineage from the higher

---

[96] "The Lemniscatory Path System – An evolution of the Copernican worldview based on statements and sketches by Rudolf Steiner on the planetary movement", Publisher Books on Demand (BoD), Norderstedt (Germany).

spiritual world, so that at our next birth we receive those hereditary factors that we need for our new physical body.

"Long before a human being enters into physical existence there is a mysterious connection between himself and the whole line of his ancestors. And the reason why specific characteristics appear in a line of ancestors is that perhaps only after hundreds of years a particular individual is to be born from that ancestral line. This human being who is to be born, perhaps centuries later, from a line of ancestors, regulates their characteristics from the spiritual world."[97]

This happens during the prenatal descent from the 5th region of the spiritual world on. We then build over a prolonged period of time and in collaboration with the higher spiritual beings, the spiritual archetype of our future head.

"The human head in its structure is such a lofty image of the universe, that the human being would be unable to form it, even with the aid of that life-wisdom which is woven into us; we would be unable to prepare it for the next incarnation. All the divine Hierarchies must cooperate in this work. Your head, this by the occiput slightly interrupted and somewhat transformed sphere, is a real microcosm, a true image of the great world-sphere. Within it lives together everything that lives outside, in the universe. Within it work together all the forces that are active in the different Hierarchies. And when we begin to shape our next incarnation, from out of the wisdom which we have collected in a process that we have grown tired of, all the Hierarchies cooperate and influence this activity, in order to embody into us, as an image of the whole wisdom of the Gods, what afterwards becomes our head.

---

[97] GA 141 "Das Leben zwischen Tod und neuer Geburt im Verhältnis zu den kosmischen Tatsachen" (Life between Death and New Birth in Relation to the Cosmic Facts), Berlin, lecture of February 11, 1913.

While all this is taking place, our physical, hereditary stream is being prepared generations ahead, here upon the earth. Just as after our death we can only hand over to the earth what comes from the earth, so we receive from our parents and forebears only that part of our being which pertains to the earth. Our earthly part is merely our exterior, it is merely the external expression within this earthly aspect."[98]

We ourselves contribute to the spiritual archetype and the physical hereditary factors of our future body, into which we move as a soul-spiritual being after conception. The knowledge of this prenatal activity remains hidden in the subconscious of most people. From the age of 49, however, when the experiences from the sphere of the spirit-self begin to be mirrored in earthly life, it occasionally penetrates up into the consciousness in the form of an inkling and then often finds expression in an increasing interest in one's ancestors. Some people carry on an avid ancestor research in the following years without being cognizant of the deeper impulses behind their interest.

An example of a different kind is provided by Rudolf Steiner's description of his contemporary Hermann Bahr, an Austrian writer who lived from 1863 to 1934. Hermann Bahr could not find access to spiritual science during Rudolf Steiner's lifetime. Nevertheless, as a person who remained capable of development throughout his life and as a seeker of the spirit, he came to the realization, in the course of his encounter with the expressionism in art, that there must exist a spiritual, inner seeing. This insight opened up to him the possibility for a deeper understanding of Goethe. That happened in his 53rd year of life. Only after the influence of the spirit-self from the higher spiritual

---

98 GA 168 "Die Verbindung zwischen Lebenden und Toten" (The Connection between the Living and the Dead), Leipzig, lecture of February 22, 1916.

world had increased sufficiently in the course of his 8th seven-year period up to its fifth year, rose Hermann Bahr to a first, delicate breakthrough of the spirit. Rudolf Steiner describes it in the following:

"Today we are only at the stage of mere groping toward this reality. In one of our recent talks I told you that a person like Hermann Bahr, a man I often met with in my youth, is seeking now — at the age of fifty-three and after having written much — to understand Goethe. Groping his way through Goethe's works, he admits that he is only just beginning to really understand Goethe and, on the other hand, is beginning to realize the fact that there is such a thing as spiritual science in addition to the physical sciences." [99]

What a wonderful example of a different kind of influence of the spirit-self sphere on the course of earthly life.

The 9th Seven-Year Period and the Sphere of the Germ Sheath of the Life Spirit (Age: 56 – 63 Years)

With the entrance into the higher spiritual world during life after death, the consciousness of even those who have been able to maintain it up to then, is slowly beginning to wan, because from then on the forces of the distant cosmos, needed for the consctruction of a healthy new earthly body, must be able to flow into us undisturbed.

"And further and further we expand into cosmic space, in continuous enlargement. But as we move out beyond the Saturn sphere our state of

[99] GA 169 "Weltwesen und Ichheit" (World-Being and I-ness), Berlin, lectures of June 20 and June 6, 1916.

consciousness is changed. We enter into a kind of cosmic twilight. We cannot call it cosmic sleep, but a cosmic twilight. Through this, however, the forces of the whole cosmos can work upon us. From all sides the forces then work upon us and we receive forces of the whole cosmos into our being. So, after we have expanded into the spheres, there is a period between death and rebirth when the forces of the whole cosmos stream into our being as from all sides, as from all stars." [100]

However, there are also human souls who are not subject to this dimming of consciousness in the higher spiritual world. These are spirit disciples who have already attained a level of initiation. Rudolf Steiner expressly emphasized in this regard:

"Unless an initiation took place in the preceding earth life, consciousness is definitely dimmed." [101]

Every initiation, even self-initiation of a low grade through meditation and concentration, brings about changes not only in the astral body, but beyond that also in the etheric body. Many people of the present time are already working on the transformation of their astral body into the spirit-self, as their I struggles for dominion over their emotions and desires, so that one is no longer driven by one's own soul life, but exerts control over it. The I then becomes the ruler of the soul. Through its ability to bring the soul to rest, the I is able to have supersensory perceptions during meditation. The spirit can then be mirrored in the soul like the light of the moon on a still surface of water. Even outside of meditation times, the soul then gradually becomes more receptive to inspirations from higher worlds.

---

[100] GA 140 "Okkulte Untersuchungen über das Leben zwischen Tod und neuer Geburt" (Occult Investigations on Life between Death and New Birth), Munich, lecture of November 26, 1912.

[101] Ibidem, Milan (Italy), lecture of October 27, 1912.

If we cultivate deeply felt religious feelings in our soul, they not only affect our astral body, but also penetrate to the etheric body. There they stimulate its transformation into life spirit. This happens in a fully conscious way during the course of spirit discipleship. For this, the disciple must acquire the ability to change his habits and character traits rooted in the etheric body. In the process one's conscience also undergoes an intensification.

"Religion is a powerful means for the purification and ennoblement of the ether body. This is the grand mission of religious impulses in the development of mankind. What is called conscience is nothing but the result of the work of the I on the life body during a series of embodiments. When man realizes that he should not do this or that, and when through this insight such a strong impression is made on him that it is propagated into his ether body, then conscience arises." [102]

By working on the etheric or life body, the spirit disciple acquires, during life on earth, a kinship with the 6th region of the spiritual world or the sphere of the germ sheath of the life spirit. When such is the case, his consciousness need no longer be dimmed during life after death, since it no longer hinders the influx of forces from the spirit-cosmos to the degree as is the case when no conscious transformation of the life body into life spirit took place in the preceding earthly life.

The religious feeling already played a role in the Jupiter sphere, or the 2nd region of the spiritual world which is is the lower counterpart to the 6th region. Likewise, the 1st region is the lower counterpart to the 7th region, and the 3rd region to the 5th region. In Figure 15, these mutual relationships are indicated by double-headed arrows.

---

102 GA 34 "Lucifer-Gnosis 1903 – 1908", essay "Die Erziehung des Kindes vom Gesichtspunkte der Geisteswissenschaft" (Education of the Child from the Point of View of Spiritual Science).

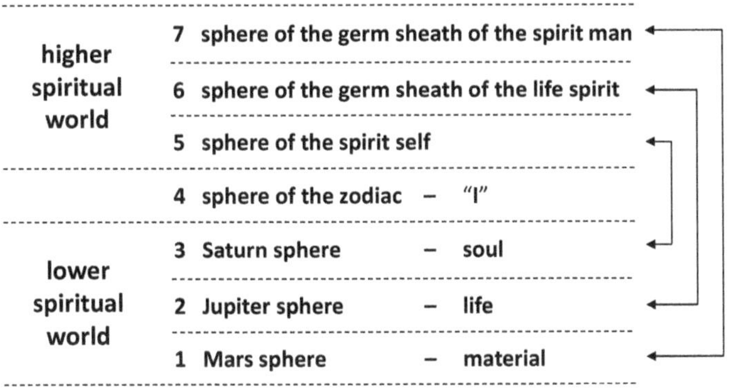
higher spiritual world
7 sphere of the germ sheath of the spirit man
6 sphere of the germ sheath of the life spirit
5 sphere of the spirit self
4 sphere of the zodiac – "I"
lower spiritual world
3 Saturn sphere – soul
2 Jupiter sphere – life
1 Mars sphere – material

Figure 15: The seven regions of the spirit world and their mutual relationships

The three highest members of the human being, the spirit-self, life spirit and spirit man, are representatives of the divine trinity. The spirit-self (Manas) is the expression of the Holy Spirit, the life spirit (Budhi or Buddhi) is the expression of the Son, and the spirit man (Atma) is the expression of the Father.

The Son said about Himself through Jesus Christ: *"I am the way, the truth and the life"* (John 14:6). He is the spirit of life or the life spirit. In nature, it expresses itself in rhythms of growth and decay, expansion and contraction, in ascending and descending. This is encompassed not only in the daily rhythms of the rising and setting sun, dawn and dusk, or in the annual rhythm of the earth's vegetation due to warmth and cold, its blossoming and withering and, ultimately in the contraction of the plant's forces into tiny seeds, but also in great rhythms such as in the century-long cycles of the human being between death and rebirth, the incarnation cycle with its rhythm of expansion of the human soul-spiritual being out into the vastness of the cosmos and its subsequent contraction until its entry into a tiny germ cell in the womb of the mother.

When in the 9th seven-year period, i.e., at the age of 56 to 63 years, the pre-natal experiences from the sphere of the germ sheath of the life spirit are mirrored in earthly life, the interest for the developmental steps b e t w e e n the incarnations, and thus for the entire human incarnation cycle, can be aroused in those who themselves feel an after-effect of their sojourn in this sphere.

The author was given to experience such. In his preceding 8th seven-year period he had little interest in the existence between the two incarnations. Then, the question of the previous embodiment was in the center of his soul life. This only changed with the transition into his 9th seven-year period, at the age of 56. Gradually the interest awoke in him for his existence in the higher worlds between his last incarnation and the present earth life, thus for the entire incarnation cycle.

In the light of this underlying diverse soul-mood of the new seven-year period, the author succeeded, through meditative contemplation of the weekly verses of the Anthroposophical Soul Calendar, in recognizing their connection with the individual stages of the human incarnation cycle. Indeed this cycle as a whole is the spiritual archetype on which the Soul Calendar is based, and it has its external expression in the week-to-week changes of nature's moods.

In the second half of the 9th seven-year period, his findings had finally matured to the point that he could set them in writing. This had not been possible in the period before, because then his soul still lacked the influence of the prenatal existence in the sphere of the germ sheath of the life spirit which only appears in the 9th seven-year period of earthly life.

Due to external circumstances, the publication of his book "The Anthroposophical Soul Calendar and the Incarnation Cycle of Man" was delayed until the 6th year of the 9th seven-year period and thus, without any special intention on the part of the author, exactly until that year which, in all seven-year periods, has a special relationship to the sixth member of the human being, the life spirit, as already has been shown schematically in figure 13 on page 104.

Likewise, the author would not have been able to write the present book "The Mirroring of Life before Birth in the Seven-Years Periods of Life on Earth" before his 9th seven-year period. For this task the impetus from the sixth region of the spiritual world, the sphere of the germ sheath of the life spirit, was necessary, too.

Thus, it becomes apparent that the individual seven-year periods of life on earth give us access to insights of a very different kind. Viewed from the outside, only the first three seven-year periods are clearly different from each other since they are associated with strong physical changes during childhood and adolescence. But all of the following seven-year periods are also connected with changes, although these are less noticeable outwardly, because the corresponding processes take place inwardly, in the life of the soul. Rudolf Steiner's words on the I-development of the human being are thus fully confirmed:

"Regarding the individual human being, we know that his I-development takes place slowly and gradually. Certainly, it is in tender infancy, from the time on to which memory reaches back, that the consciousness of the I begins. But this I progressively ripens and progresses in its development. Significant errors exist in our time in regard to the development of this I. There is far too little awareness of the fact that such an I-development is taking place in life. And so we may experience that today people in their greenest youth find themselves mature to

judge everything, because they don't know that at first a certain age has to be reached to be able to judge certain things, because it is only then that the I has reached a certain maturity." [103]

To this effect, it is of great importance to preserve one's ability to develop, even with increasing age. Secondly, the degree of consciousness with which we passed through the higher worlds between our last death and new birth plays a major role. The lower its degree, the duller the consciousness, the greater the degree of the mirroring of the spheres taking place in our subconscious. The differences between the seven-year periods thus penetrate only sparsely into the consciousness. However, one can have a beneficial effect on this by examining one's own course of life more closely to see how the focal points of interest and the basic mood of the soul have changed from one seven-year period to the next, and also how certain questions in the soul life have come to the fore at various times.

A natural connection with the sphere of the germ sheath of the life spirit was probably still attained by the ancient Mongols. In his statements about the "getting younger" of mankind Rudolf Steiner mentions only the post-Atlantean cultures.[104] But if one lets his description of the Mongols in the final age of the Atlantean epoch, before the great flood catastrophe, to have an effect, one gets the impression that their soul-spiritual ripening extended seven years beyond that of the primeval post-Atlantean Indians, namely up to the age of 56 to 63 years, therefore, up to the 9th seven-year period.

As with all Atlanteans, the memory of the deeds and lineage of their ancestors played a prominent role among the ancient Mongols. Accordingly, there was a pronounced ancestor worship among all

---

[103] GA 159 "Das Geheimnis des Todes" (The mystery of Death), Nuremberg, lecture of March 14, 1915.

[104] See page 70 f.

Atlantean peoples. But it also seems that in old age the Mongols became especially receptive to the influence from the sphere of the germ sheath of the life spirit, for they revered the life force as the supremely important divine power. It is possible that they still matured naturally up to the years of the 9th seven-year period. Rudolf Steiner said the following about them:

"They remained true to their sense of memory. And so they came to the conclusion that the most ancient must also be the wisest, must be that which could best defend itself against the power of thought. They had indeed lost the command of the life-force, but that which developed in them as thought-power had in itself something of the natural power of this life-force. It is true, they had lost the power over life, but never the direct, instinctive belief in the life-force. This force had become to them their God on whose behalf they performed everything which they considered right. Thus, they appeared to their neighbours to be possessed of this secret power, and they yielded to it in blind faith. Their descendants in Asia and in some European regions showed, and still show, much of this peculiarity." [105]

This, then, is the reason why contemporary Mongolians and Chinese continue to pay such close attention to the life force. Today, they call it Chi or Qi (pronounced: chee) and often practice the art of movement, the Tai Chi, together in large groups in public in order to release blockages in the body so as to release the free flow of life energy. In Chinese medicine, they use acupuncture or moxibustion[106] to ensure that Chi can flow freely again along the meridians, the energetic flow paths of the body.

---

105 GA 11 "Aus der Akasha-Chronik" (From the Akasha Chronicle), chapter "Unsere atlantischen Vorfahren" (Our Atlantean Ancestors).

106 The heating of certain points on the body.

At the time of the Mongolian subrace of ancient Atlantis, the vernal equinox passed through the zodiacal region of Leo. In it rules the sun, which gives life to all creatures of the earth. The sun is the physical expression of the life spirit in the sky. It is true that the Mongols could not experience the sun as brightly as we do today, because at that time the sky was still almost constantly cloudy and the sunlight penetrated only dimly through the dense clouds. Only with the great flood or the ice age at the end of the Atlantean epoch, the dense cloud cover gradually rained and snowed down into the ocean basins and on the continents, so that breaks in the cloud occasionally allowed a clear view of the blue sky.

Instead of the physical rays of light, however, the late Atlantean Mongols perceived, by means of their ancient clairvoyance, the life-rays of the sun, its etheric rays, the bearers of the life force. It is these, which they worshiped as divine power.

The 10th Seven-Year Period and the Sphere of the Germ Sheath of the Spirit Man (Age: 63 – 70 Years)

With the 63rd birthday begins that period of seven-years in earthly life in which the seventh and highest region of the spiritual world is mirrored. In the existence between two incarnations this high sphere can be lived through in fully consciousness only by the masters. They find here the spiritual germ sheath of the spirit man or Atma, the seventh and highest of the human members, witch has its home on the Atmic plane, the divine world of the Father. It is from this lofty plane above the Budhi plane or the world of the Son, that he works into the highest sphere of the spiritual world.

Once people will have learned to transform at least a part of their physical bodies through conscious spiritual activity into Atma, the spirit man, or at least into its preliminary stage, as far as this is possible during the course of earth evolution, they will have reached the stage of the masters and thus will be able to experience in full consciousness the highest region of the spiritual world. Until then, these experiences remain hidden in the subconscious or in the depths of the unconscious from where they exert their effects. In Rudolf Steiner's words:

"When man has arrived at the border of the three worlds, he recognizes himself in his own life-kernel. This implies that for him the riddles of these three worlds have been solved. Thus, he has a complete view of the entire life of these worlds. In the physical life the capacities of the soul, through which it obtains the experiences in the spiritual world here described, remain unconscious under ordinary circumstances. They work in its unconscious depths upon the bodily organs which bring about the consciousness of the physical world." [107]

The "three worlds" Rudolf Steiner speaks of here are the physical world, the soul world and the spiritual world. It is within these that people develop the consciousness of themselves, the I-consciousness. For the vast majority of the people this is possible only during the waking state in the physical world. Soon after falling asleep, as the astral body and the I begin to loosen their connection with the etheric and physical body, we enter into a dream state, and finally sink into an entirely unconscious state of deep sleep. But in the course of future incarnations on earth we will gradually gain the ability to maintain our I-consciousness and to be able to act consciously even in the out-of-

---

[107] GA 9 "Theosophie", chapter "Der Geist im Geisterland nach dem Tode" (The Spirit in the Land of Spirits after death).

body existence during the dream and sleep state. We are, after all, cosmic spirit-beings, and it is the task of Anthroposophy to make us fully aware of this fact. That is why Rudolf Steiner begins the first of his "Guiding Principles" with the words: *"Anthroposophy is a path of knowledge which seeks to lead the spiritual in the human being to the spiritual in the universe."* [108]

In contrast to the animals which, unconscious of themselves, live on earth mainly as instinct-driven s o u l -beings, dreaming and sleeping away most of the time of the day, humans experience themselves for about two thirds of the twenty-four hour period as self-conscious awake s p i r i t -beings. The human being is thus the representative of the spiritual world on earth. Accordingly, one's earthly life is primarily under the influence of the prenatal experiences in the spiritual world.

Our childhood and youth are still predominantly influenced by our prenatal experiences in the higher soul world. However, as soon as we mature into adulthood and become fully responsible for our actions, we come under the direct influence of the spiritual world. Therefore, the time from the 21st to the 70th year of life can be divided exactly into seven seven-year periods which correspond to the seven regions or spheres of the spiritual world. Figure 16 shows how these spheres, from the Mars sphere to the sphere of the germ sheath of the spirit man, are mirrored exactly in the seven-year periods in which we spend most of our life as active adults.

Between the ages of 63 and 70, most people end their professional working life. This means that the years of "duty" end and a period of freer and more independent life begins. Some continue to work part-time for a while to make the transition to retirement less abrupt. After

[108] GA 26 "Anthroposophische Leitsätze" (Anthroposophical Leading Principles)

that, it is up to each individual what he or she makes of the following period of life, whether the free time is used for spiritual development or one merely indulges in pleasure and pursues trivialities.

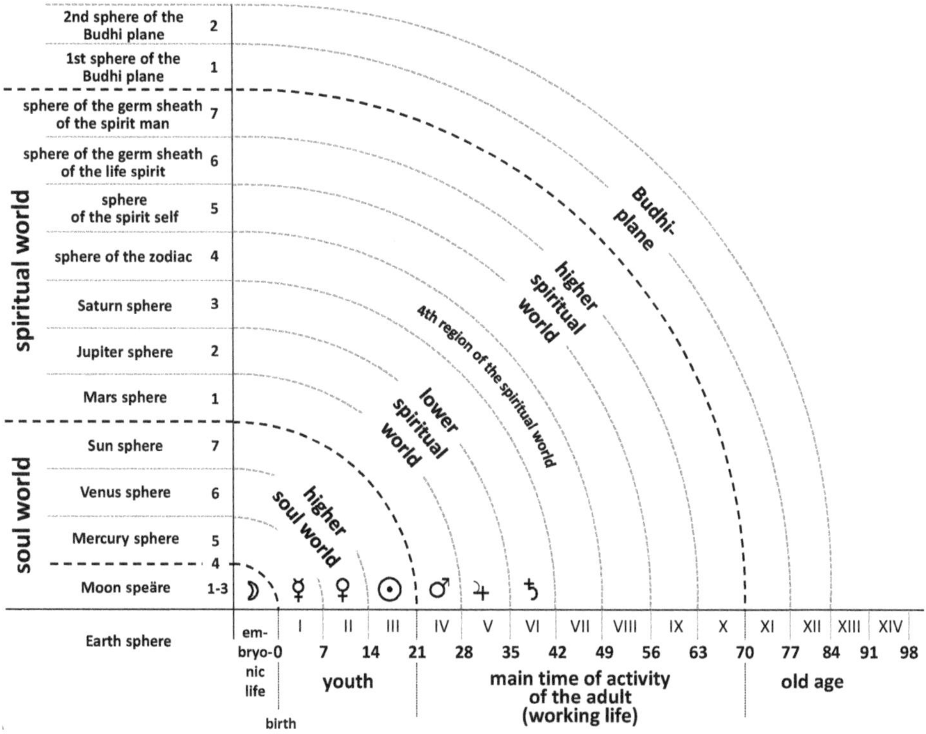

Figure 16:
Overview of the mirroring of life before birth in the 7-year periods of life on earth

At this point, the author would like to relate an experience that befell him after he had already finished writing this book. While the above illustration had been completed several weeks before, the proofreading and final formatting for printing still needed to be done. It so happened that in the middle of June 2022, the Rudolf Steiner Verlag in Switzerland drew attention by e-mail to the publication of the wonderful large picture biography "Rudolf Steiner (1861 - 1925)". The book contains about 500 pages. When the author took a curious random look at the back of the book, he "accidentally" opened the page 423. To his surprise, he saw a notebook entry by Rudolf Steiner from the spring of 1924, in which he divided his own life course into seven-year periods.

Rudolf Steiner, 63 at the time, made the following entry: *"63: Vater (father) 1924"*. In the line above he wrote *"63 – 56: Sonnengeist (Sun Spirit) 1917"* and so on, looking backwards, assigning to each seven-year period one of the seven ancient levels of initiation, down to *"28 – 21: Rabe (raven)"*. In a lecture, Rudolf Steiner explained what is meant by these degrees of initiation:

"First degree: the Raven. It denotes the one who is on the threshold. The raven appears in all mythologies. In the Edda he whispers into the ear of Wotan what he sees in the distance.

Second degree: the secret Scholar, or Occultist.

Third degree: the Warrior (struggle, strife).

Fourth degree: the Lion (strength).

Fifth degree: the initiate bears the name of the people to which he belongs: Persian or Greek, because his soul has extended to his whole people.

Sixth degree: Sun-Hero or Sun-Messenger, because his course has become as harmonious, as rhythmic as the course of the sun. The sun represented the rhythmic, living movement of the planetary system. [...]

Seventh degree: the Father, because he has now become capable of schooling disciples and of being the protector of all humans; and since he is the father of the new human being, born for a second time in the awakened soul." [109]

Each of these degrees of initiation corresponds to one of the seven regions of the spiritual world. Rudolf Steiner's assignment of the degrees of initiation to the seven seven-year periods before the age of 70 is consequently a clear confirmation of the representation in Figure 16 (page 135). The relevant notebook entry by Rudolf Steiner was previously unknown to the author. So he felt it as a fortunate coincidence and surprising confirmation of his own findings when this information was made available to him immediately after he had finished writing the present book and just in time for him to insert a short report about it before the book was sent off for printing.

Only at the age of 21 to 28 years the direct access to the spiritual world opens to us, initially to its first region, the Mars sphere. With it Rudolf Steiner connects the initiation degree of the Raven. In the ancient mystery schools the Raven was responsible for the contact with the outer physical world.

At the age of 28 to 35 we become receptive to influences from the second region of the spiritual world, the Jupiter sphere. It is related to religious feeling, by which is meant true spiritual religiosity. The spirit disciple immerses himself in the study of esoteric teachings. In our time, these can be found in esoteric Christianity and the cosmology connected with it. The corresponding ancient degree of initiation was that of the student of occult teachings, the Occultist.

When we become receptive to the Saturn sphere at the age of 35 to 42, we feel the inner impulse to external activity. We want to stand up

---

109 GA 94 "Kosmogonie" (Cosmogony), Paris (France), lecture of May 30, 1906.

for our spiritual ideals in the outer world, to translate them into outer deeds. This corresponds to the Warrior's degree of initiation.

At the age of 42 to 49, we are challenged to stand entirely on our own two feet and demonstrate inner strength. This degree correspondes to the Lion and is related to the zodiacal sphere, the fourth and middle region of the spiritual world.

The next three seven-year periods give us access to the three regions of the higher spiritual world. In them, the three divine beings are expressed: the Holy Spirit, in the fifth region, the Son in the sixth, and the Father in the seventh.

The region of the Holy Spirit is also the sphere of the spirit-self. Between the ages of 49 and 56, in the 8th seven-year period, we are particularly receptive to it and it is during this time that we may be given insights into our past incarnations. We then identify not only with our present I, but also with another one, perhaps even with three or more past "I"s. In case of advanced spirit disciples, the possibility exists that they identify with all members of their nation. Then the initiate bears the name of his people.

The sixth degree is the Son, Sun Hero or Sun-Messenger. It is the initiation stage of the sixth region of the spirit world, the sphere of the germ sheath of the life spirit. At this stage one attains the understanding of the rhythms of life. Rudolf Steiner assigned it to the age of 56 to 63, the 9th seven-year period.

And whoever attains the degree of the Father has gained access to the seventh and highest region of the spirit world. It corresponds to the age of 63 to 70, or the 10th seven-year period.

Hence, the author's description in Figure 16 (page 135) finds its explicit confirmation in Rudolf Steiner's notebook entry.

Thus, we are given to understand that what humanity lost through "getting younger" as it progressed through the ages from one seven-year period to another, could be regained within the ancient Mysteries through schooling and special initiations.

Should anyone wish to continue his or her development well until the 10th seven-year period it behoves him or her to remain mentally active throughout life and deal with spiritual matters, such as are available to us in an exemplary way through Anthroposophy.

Our considerations in the preceding chapter have shown that Rudolf Steiner's statements about the "getting younger" of mankind can be extended back to the last age of the Atlantean civilization, that of the Mongols. The late-Atlantean Mongols continued to mature soul-spiritually up to the age of 56 to 63 and thus became receptive to the influences from the sixth region of the spiritual world, the sphere of the germ sheath of the Life Spirit. Therefore, the life-force was the highest divine principle which they worshipped. If such was the case, should we not be allowed to assume that during the preceding age the Akkadians, the second to last subrace of the Atlanteans, could possibly still mature naturally up to the age of 63 to 70 years, and thereby come into contact with the paternal sphere of the germ sheath of the Spirit Man, the seventh and highest region of the spiritual world?

Let us remember what Rudolf Steiner wrote about the after-death passage through this sphere in his book "Theosophy": *""When man has arrived at the border of the three worlds, he recognizes himself in his own life-kernel. This implies that the riddles of these three worlds have been solved to him. Thus, he has a complete view of the entire life of these worlds."*[110]

---

110 GA 9 "Theosophie" (Theosophy), chapter "Der Geist im Geisterland nach dem Tode" (The Spirit in the Land of Spirits in Life after Death).

This overview of the three worlds, within which humanity develops, allows a deep insight into the order of the individual spheres as well as into the laws, according to which everything is arranged and structured. At the time of the ancient Akkadians, the vernal equinox moved through the zodiacal region of Virgo, from which primarily ordering and structuring forces emanate. Possibly this is the reason why the Akkadians did not regulate their social coexistence from memory, but tried to impose a mental order on everything and even extend this to other peoples and countries.

Unfortunately, only scant information about the late-Atlantean Akkadians has been given to us by Rudolf Steiner. But even from what he did convey it is evident that they were a strong-willed people in whom the father principle was expressed, which is intimately connected with the sphere of the germ sheath of the spirit man. The manifold and often contradictory will impulses of the Akkadians required a strict regulation. For this purpose, they used the power of thinking, which had already been developing since the fifth Atlantean subrace, the primeval Semites, in order to establish a spirit- and thought-based legal order, different from the previously more soul-based one, still relying on memory. This new thought-based order of the Akkadians appears to have been of a similarly stern nature as the later law order of Moses, who demanded from his people an obedience and a subordination such as a domineering father would demand from his children. With the Akkadians, the power of thinking and the power of will worked together.

"However, under the influence of the power of thought, a love of novelty and a longing for change were developed. Everyone wanted to carry out what his own sagacity suggested; and thus, it is that restlessness begins to appear in the fifth sub-race, leading in the sixth [the Akkadians] to the fact that they felt the need of placing under general laws the capricious ideas of the single individual. The glory

of the states of the third sub-race lay in the order and harmony caused by a common memory. In the sixth this order had to be brought about by deliberately constructed laws. Thus, in the sixth sub-race must be sought the origin of l a w a n d l e g i s l a t i o n.

And during the third sub-race the segregation of a group of human beings took place only when in a manner they were compelled to leave, because they no longer felt comfortable within the prevailing conditions, brought about by recollection. It was essentially different in the sixth. The calculating power of thought sought novelty as such; it urged them to enterprise and new establishments. Thus, the Akkadians were an enterprising people inclined towards colonization. It was commerce especially that fed the young and germinating power of thought and judgment."[111]

Mercury, the ruler in the force region of the zodiacal image[112] of Virgo, not only governs thought and the exchange of ideas, but has also been worshipped as the protector of travellers and the god of commerce.

The will power, however, on which the development of the Spirit Man is based, is under the providence of the Father-God. The world was created according to his guidelines and his will in cooperation with the Son-God. Therefore, Christ taught us to pray, *"Our Father in heaven, ... Thy w i l l be done on earth as it is in the heaven."* And even during the difficult trials in the Garden of

---

111 GA 11 "Aus der Akasha-Chronik" (From the Akasha Chronicle), chapter "Unsere atlantischen Vorfahren" (Our Atlantean Ancestors).

112 The zodiacal *images* which people of the ancient cultures saw in the soul by means of the old clairvoyance, are not congruent with the zodiacal *signs* or the physically visible *constellations*. For more details see e.g. the book "Influences of the Forces of the Zodiac on the Cultural Development of Mankind" by Roland Schrapp.

Gethsemane, on the eve of crucifixion, Christ Jesus prayed to him, *"Yet not my will, but thy will be done."* (Luke 22:42)

In the world of gods of the Akkadians, the father principle seems to have played a special role. Their descendants at the time of the Sumerians worshipped Enlil, as the "king of heaven and earth" and as the "father of the gods". His title later passed to lower deities, such as the Greek Zeus, who was also called the father of the gods. However, the ancient Greeks, like the ancient Akkadians, knew that there were still higher deities, although they were less accessible to them.

The question arises, how the connection with the highest region of the spiritual world can be expressed in the 10th seven-year period of everyday people, who are not masters, and experience life after death only with "dimmed" consciousness? Naturally, the author cannot give any reliable information about this from his own life experience. Besides, he was only 65 years old at the time when he wrote this book, and, accordingly, was only in the third year of his 10th seven-year period. Furthermore, in each seven-year period, only the seventh and last year is in intimate connection with the spirit man, the highest member of our being, which today exists only in a seed-like condition (cf. Figure 13, page 104). A retrospective evaluation of the experiences in the 10th seven-year period regarding a possible influence from the 7th region of the spiritual world can therefore only take place after the completion of the 70th year.

But perhaps the author owes the possibility of being able to write the present book in his 10th seven-year period already due to the influence from the seventh region of the spiritual world, since the content of the book does not only deal with the order of the earthly course of life according to seven-year periods, but in particular with the stages of development of the human consciousness.

Doesn't this remind us of Rudolf Steiner's statement quoted above, according to which we receive an overview of all three worlds in the highest region of the spiritual world? Possibly, it is only on account of this that we gain the full overview of the individual steps of the development of consciousness of mankind within the three worlds. In any case, Rudolf Steiner pointed out in his own handwritten note for Édouard Schuré in May 1906, that in Christian esotericism the states of consciousness are called Father, the states of life Son, and the states of form Holy Spirit.[113] The seven states of consciousness which humanity has to pass through within the three worlds, from ancient Saturn in the distant past to Vulcan in the distant future, are therefore external expressions of the Father principle. And it is on this basic principle of the number 7 that the seven-year periods in human life on earth are based.

The overview described in this book and the examples given of the gradual development of consciousness from one seven-year period to the next are, of course, only a fragment in comparison to what is experienced by those, who can consciously perceive experiences in the seventh region of the spiritual world. However, Rudolf Steiner also pointed out that influences from that region work into our subconscious during our earthly life. And those who follow the path of spirit discipleship will soon find that the misty veil which conceals the contents of our subconscious from our daytime consciousness gradually becomes thinner and more "porous", so that one thing or another does percolate into consciousness, even if initially only to a small degree.

---

113 GA 89 "Bewusstsein – Leben – Form" (Consciousness – Life – Form), chapter "Zeichen und Entwicklung der drei Logoi in der Menschheit" (Signs and Development of the Three Logoi in Mankind).

In addition, it must be considered that every sincere meditant is allowed to participate during sleep in nocturnal teachings by the masters in the supersensory mystery school led by Christian Rosenkreutz. As time goes by, the content of these lessons will gradually penetrate into consciousness and become clearer and more comprehensive the morning after.

"Meditating, means to open the soul to the master that he can give it impulses at night. The astral body receives lessons unconsciously at first. This will gradually become more and more conscious. In the beginning, incursions into day consciousness, which cannot be explained, later day-consciousness and higher consciousness at the same time. – St. G. [St. Germain][114] *teaches Theosophy in such a way that it meets the demands of the educated European*[115]*. [He] is now the most important master."* [116]

Fact is, however, that many of those who are not yet attracted to walk the path of spirit discipleship may discover an inclination, after their retirement, to look back on their life in an attempt to bring order into the manifold memories, and to trace hidden laws in the soul-spiritual course of one's own development of consciousness.

---

114 This refers to Christian Rosenkreutz, of whom Rudolf Steiner said: *"The Count of Saint-Germain was the same personality who in previous incarnation founded the Order of the Rosicrucians."* GA 93 "Die Tempellegende und die Goldene Legende" (The Temple Legend and the Golden Legend), Berlin, lecture of November 4, 1904.

115 including people of European origin on other continents

116 GA 266c "Aus den Inhalten der esoterischen Stunden" (From the Contents of the Esoteric Lessons), Vol. III, Berlin, esoteric lesson of March 18, 1906.

The 11th Seven-Year Period and the First Sphere of the Budhi plane (Age: 70 – 77 Years)

When a person turns 70 years old, he or she has reached the natural limit of his or her life on earth, because the human being consists of 10 members[117], and during earthly life we are granted periods of seven years for the further development of each of these members. Thus, after 10 x 7 = 70 years this period naturally comes to an end. What we have worked out in our prenatal existence in cooperation with higher beings and prepared for our life on earth, could develop step by step during the 10 seven-year periods. The pre-natal experiences in the different spheres of the higher worlds were therewith given sufficient opportunity to find their expression in earthly life.

Also the part of our karma from the past, which we were supposed to have worked off during our earthly life, will have largely been fulfilled by the age of 70. Any additional years are a "bestowal of grace" from that world which lies above the spiritual world, a gift from the Budhi plane, from the world of life spirit or the Christ. In one of the karma lectures, Rudolf Steiner once commented on this as follows:

"This study of karma makes us altogether aware of the connections between human life here upon earth and that which goes on in the wide universe. We see this human life taking its course on earth, unfolding till about the 70th year of life, when in a certain connection it attains its limit. Whatever lies beyond this is in reality a life given by grace. What lies below this limit stands under karmic influences." [118]

---

117 The threefold body, the threefold soul, the "I", and the threefold spirit

118 GA 237 "Esoterische Betrachtungen karmischer Zusammenhänge – Band III" (Karmic Relationships – Vol. 3), Dornach, lecture of July 6, 1924.

This statement could be interpreted to mean that after the age of 70 we can no longer be affected by any painful karma caused by ourselves in previous lives. But this would probably be too narrow an interpretation of Rudolf Steiner's words, because we know from many other of his statements that they only describe the rule. However, there are individual exceptions. Thus, the principle of "no rule without exception" also applies here.

As far as the occurrence of diseases in old age is concerned, one must certainly distinguish at least three types. On the one hand, there are diseases that are simply the natural consequence of an unhealthy lifestyle in the present life.

Furthermore, there are diseases in old age, which only work to enable us to pass through the gate of death. They are, so to speak, the door openers for this gate and serve our liberation from the physical body, which has grown old and has now become an obstacle for further soul-spiritual development. A loosening from the body at a natural death is therefore experienced by the deceased with a feeling of immense relief and greatest bliss.

A third group of diseases in old age are those which are neither karmic nor the result of an unhealthy way of life but represent a "first cause" through which we may earn a positive karmic compensation in the future life. Such diseases may occur at any ages. However, they are likely to occur more frequently after the age of 70, in the "grace" period of life.

"As with all things concerning the human being, so also in regard to health and illness, the matter must not be conceived as if they were simply «punishment» and «reward» for what a human being has committed in a former, or perhaps even in «this» life. For example, a person can be afflicted with an illness of which no cause can be proven, neither in the previous nor in the present life. Then the illness occurs, so

to speak, as a «first» event in the course of the human life, it is a «first» cause. It will then exert its effect in some way in the following life."[119]

About the real causes of our diseases in earthly life we will receive complete enlightenment only when passing through the sphere of Mercury in the life after death.[120]

Notwithstanding the above, we can be affected by harsh and painful experiences in old age as part of the general karma of the people or even of mankind. This may happen, for example, in the case of catastrophes caused by war or famine. In such cases, entire groups of people can be affected and it is rarely a matter of individual karma.

It is by the grace of Christ that additional years of life are given to us. He is the Lord of Karma as well as the Lord of the life forces, he is the Spirit of Life, which surrounds us as the life spirit or Budhi and will increasingly penetrate us in the future. By the time we reach the age of 70, we begin to become even more receptive to it than in the years prior. We then look back on the life we have spent on earth up to that point from outside the "three worlds", as it were, from a higher vantage point than was possible before.

In this respect, the years after the 70th birthday prove to be particularly suitable in order to connect oneself once again quite intensively with Christ in the twilight of life, and to bring to consciousness how this lofty being, the highest of the Sun Spirits and representative of the Son God within the creation, connected Himself with the earth and mankind at the time of the Graeco-Roman culture, in the age of Aries. Therefore, let us take a closer look at the lengthy

---

119 GA 34 "Lucifer-Gnosis", section "Wie hat man sich Gesundheit und Krankheit im Sinne des Karmagesetzes zu denken?" (How to understand health and illness in the sense of the law of karma?), 1906.

120 See page 48.

descent of the Christ spirit to the earth, from a less familiar perspective, with respect to the development of human consciousness.

Our seed of the spirit-self or Manas belongs to the higher spiritual world, the world of the Holy Spirit. However, our seed of the life spirit, the Budhi, lies in the next higher world, on the Budhi plane from where the Christ impulse emanates. Only in the distant future we will be able to develop the seed of the spirit man or Atma, which is rooted in the lofty Atmic Plane, the world of the Father. Today these three highest members of the human being are still at a rudimentary stage of development.

Already in ancient Lemuria, the preliminary stage of the spirit-self could be connected with our astral body, because at that time a part of the astral body was already transformed into the sentient soul which could serve as a connecting link to the seed of the spirit-self. This connection was though still only rudimentary and very loose.

However, the humans of ancient Lemuria were not at all capable of absorbing the seed of the Budhi. Even in the following Atlantic epoch the necessary conditions for this were not given. The Budhi only hovered over the people but it could not yet enter into them. From then on, Christ, the highest of the Sun Spirits, prepared the people so that they would be able to receive the Budhi during the course of the following fifth great epoch or the post-Atlantean epoch. Rudolf Steiner gave the following explanation:

"For the whole earth there was a common spirit who could pour out over the entire mankind with all its members the element of the Sun Spirits or Fire Spirits, the Budhi or the life spirit. However, during the Lemurian race and in the Atlantean period, humans were not yet mature enough to receive anything from this Sun Spirit. In the Akasha Chronicle, a strange phenomenon can be observed, namely, that humans at the time consisted of physical body, etheric body, astral body, and of

the spirit-self. But the spirit-self was indwelling the humans only very slightly. The Budhi or life spirit hovered around everyone, but this was perceivable only in the astral space. Everyone was surrounded by Budhi in the astral space; but this Budhi, which hovered around the human beings on the outside, was not yet ripe to enter them. It was a part of the one great Fire Spirit who had poured out his drops upon the human beings. But they could not yet enter the people. Only through the deed of Christ on earth, the rudiments were formed by which the human beings could receive what we call Budhi into their Manas. [...]

What entered into the physical, etheric, and astral body of Jesus of Nazareth was the entirety of this Fire Spirit, the common source of all spirit sparks bestowed on humanity. This is the Christ, the only divine being, which, in this way, does not exist in any other form on earth. He entered the Jesus of Nazareth, in order that those who felt connected with the Christ Jesus received the power to absorb the Budhi into themselves. The possibility of receiving the Budhi begins with the appearance of Christ Jesus. This is what John called the divine Creator-Word. The divine Creator-Word is this Fire Spirit who poured out his sparks into the human beings." [121]

The possibility of receiving the Budhi had to be carefully prepared through a series of ages. The beginning of this development was in the time of the fifth subrace of Atlantis, when the primeval Semites developed into the most advanced part of humanity at the time. After they had passed the age of 70, they were still receptive to the influence of the Christ from the Budhi Plane, at least in so far as it emanated from the lowest or first sphere of this plane, which is related to the human physical body. Therefore, they were particularly suited in the course of their further development, to provide the necessary

---

[121] GA 97 "Das christliche Mysterium" (The Christian Mystery), Cologne, lecture of December 2, 1906.

conditions so that, in the middle of the post-Atlantean epoch, the Christ, and with him the Budhi, could enter into the physical body of a single human being, of Jesus of Nazareth. For this reason, the primeval Semites, the fifth Atlantean "subrace", were designated the "root race" for the mankind of the post-Atlantean or fifth great epoch.

In the middle of the Lemurian epoch, on account of Lucifer's intervention, human astral bodies had already been implanted with the ability to develop passions and be roused with enthusiasm over something. Consequently, until the middle of the Atlantean epoch, people developed a strong self-will as the basis of a free will. However, this will was not yet really free and independent but strongly determined by the desires and passions of the astral body. In the case of the primeval Turanians, the fourth Atlantean subrace, the self-will developed to such a destructive extent that an urgent countermeasure had to be taken in order to bring mankind back into a balance.

"Such a destructive effect could only be arrested by cultivation of a higher force in the human being. This was the power of thought. Logical thinking has a restraining effect on selfish personal wishes. We must seek the origin of the logical thinking in the fifth subrace [the primeval Semites]. People began to go beyond the simple remembrance of the past. They began to compare their various experiences. The power of judgment developed, and by this power of judgment the wishes, the desires were controlled. The human beings began to calculate, to combine. They learned to work with thoughts." [122]

The development of the power of judgment could begin with the fifth sub-race of Atlantis, because at the time, the vernal equinox moved within the range of forces of the zodiacal image of Libra, from which emanate the soul forces of weighing, comparing and judging.

---

[122] GA 11 "Aus der Akasha-Chronik" (From the Akasha Chronicle), chapter "Unsere atlantischen Vorfahren" (Our Atlantean ancestors).

For this purpose the life body or etheric body, the lower counterpart of the life spirit, had to be accordingly developed and partly transformed into the intellectual soul, which, in turn, would after a certain stage of development, serve as the link by which the rudiment of the life spirit could enter the people.

However, the intellectual soul reached the required maturity only in the middle of our post-Atlantean epoch, in the age of Aries, because only the Greeks and Romans succeeded in working their way up to a culture of the intellectual soul. In addition, the development of the I-consciousness needed to take place.

"The cultivation of the human intellect, of the consciousness of oneself, was not yet present among the Atlanteans. They lived in a kind of clairvoyance. It was only the fifth subrace of the Atlanteans, the primeval Semites, who developed the first elements of the combining mind that continued in the fifth root race. It is by this that the I-consciousness arises. The individual Atlantean did not yet say «I» or «Me» to himself with the same intensity as the members of the following age did." [123]

The physical bodies of the primeval Semites still had a strongly backward receding forehead. Their ether bodies, on the other hand, clearly protruded forward beyond the forehead of the physical body. For the development of the I-consciousness, however, it was necessary that the physical body and the ether body came closer to each other. They finally had to come to a congruence above the root of the nose.

"It was another point in time when the human being began to denote himself with the word «I». This happened in Atlantis, at the time of the

---

123 GA 92 "Die okkulten Wahrheiten alter Mythen und Sagen" (Occult Truths of Ancient Myths and Legends), Berlin, lecture of March 28, 1905.

primeval Semites, in that a certain point in the physical head joined with another in the etheric head."[124]

During the following ages, the physical forehead, which was originally slanted backward, shifted more and more forward and thus came into a more vertical position above the nasal root. This caused an increase in the perception of the outer physical world during the day and at the same time a decrease in the clairvoyant states of consciousness at night. Today we are completely without any conscious perception for the duration of deep sleep at night, but wide awake during the day, far more awake than even the people of classical antiquity. They often experienced day or waking dreams, and, on occasion, even true clairvoyant dreams.

The entire process of dimming of the ancient clairvoyance and a concomitant directing of the human perceptive faculty to the external physical world, for the purpose of development of the intellect and the I-consciousness, extended over a total of seven ages. During this time, the vernal equinox moved backward from Libra, where it was at the time of the primeval Semites, by six zodiacal images, to Aries, at the time of the Greco-Roman culture.

The seven zodiacal images, from Libra to Aries, are related to the seven macrocosmic members of the Christ. They are the seven bright images of the zodiac, those of the summer half-year, in contrast to the five dark ones of the winter half-year. Rudolf Steiner once described them in connection with the seven members of the human being.[125]

---

124 GA 94 "Kosmogonie" (Cosmogony), Munich, lecture of November 5, 1906.

125 GA 102 "Das Hereinwirken geistiger Wesenheiten in den Menschen," (The Influence of Spritual Beings upon Man) Berlin, lecture of January 27, 1908 (this lecture is now called: "Good and Evil Spirits and their Influence on Humanity")

The descent of the Christ being from the Budhi plane to Earth happened gradually. First, the zodiacal forces of Libra came into effect. Through them the primeval Semites received the first impulse for the preparation of the subsequent reception of the Budhi by the human beings. As the next preparatory stages, at the time of the Akkadians, an influx of forces from the realm of Virgo set in, with the Mongols from the realm of Leo, with the primeval Indians from the realm of Cancer, and so on until eventually, under the influence of the forces of Aries, at the time of the ancient Greeks, the intellectual soul was so far developed that it could finally serve as a link between the life body and the life spirit.

HUMAN BEING		CHRIST		
		7th	♈	Aries
		6th	♉	Taurus
		5th	♊	Gemini
		4th	♋	Cancer
		3rd	♌	Leo
7th	spirit man	2nd	♍	Virgo
6th	life spirit	1st	♎	Libra
5th	spirit self		♏	Scorpio
4th	"I"		♐	Sagittarius
3rd	astral body		♑	Capricorn
2nd	etheric body		♒	Aquarius
1st	physical body		♓	Pisces

Figure 17: The seven members of the Christ being and of the human being

At the same time, the spirit self or Manas of Jesus of Nazareth was enabled to serve as a pure vessel for the Budhi. Only then the conditions for the entry of the Christ being with the Budhi into an earthly human body were given.[126] Hence the words of Rudolf Steiner already quoted above:

"Through the deed of Christ on earth, the rudiments were formed in the human beings so that they could receive what we call Budhi into their Manas."[127]

Only since that time it is possible for us humans to work on the conscious transformation of the etheric body to Budhi through the instrument of the I.

As already mentioned, for the development of the intellectual soul as well as for the development of the I-consciousness, a turning of the human perceptive faculty to the outer physical world was necessary. This occurred simultaneously with the dimming of the old clairvoyance. Formerly experienced supersensory images of the world of the gods became progressively indistinct. The ancient Germanic peoples experienced this tragic process as "twilight of the gods". Even during life after death they were less and less able to reach the higher worlds with their dreamlike picture consciousness. And since the darkening in the spheres of the soul and the spiritual world was mirrored in the seven-year periods of life on earth, people reached the natural limit of their clairvoyance at an increasingly younger age.

---

126 What other complicated processes were necessary to prepare the unique body as well as the unique soul of Jesus of Nazareth for the reception of the Christ-Spirit, describes Rudolf Steiner amongst others, in his lecture cycles on the two Jesus children and the Gospels of Luke and of Matthew (GA 114 and GA 123).

127 GA 97 "Das christliche Mysterium" (The Christian Mystery), Cologne, lecture of December 2, 1906.

The case was rather different with the primeval Semites. They, on the contrary, were able to maintain their dreamlike image-consciousness during the after-death ascent through the spheres all the way to the first sphere of the Budhi plane. In their life on earth, this was mirrored in their souls from the age of 70 on, with the beginning of the 11th seven-year period. Thus they felt intimately connected with the Budhi or the life spirit, and could therefore receive the unique mission of contributing to the incarnation of Christ and the endowment of mankind with the Budhi.

With the late Akkadians, the ascent with the dreamlike image consciousness still took place up to the highest region of the spiritual world, up to the border of the "three worlds". Accordingly, they were still able to become naturally receptive to influences from the seventh region of the spiritual world, the sphere of the germ sheath of the spirit man, from their 10th seven-year period, between the ages of 63 and 70.

The Mongols, the last Atlantean race, could still penetrate between two incarnations with their dreamlike consciousness to the second highest region of the spiritual world, the sphere of the germ sheath of the life spirit. This was mirrored in their souls in life on earth from their 9th seven-year period, at the age of 56 to 63 years.

Thus, the people's consciousness darkened earlier and earlier after death. With each successive epoch, the ability of perception was lost for one sphere. The consciousness of the ancient Indians still reached to the sphere of the spirit self, the fifth region of the spiritual world. Thus, at the age of 49 to 56, they could still look back on their past incarnations.

The ancient Persians still had access to the sphere of the zodiac, the Egyptians, Chaldeans and Babylonians up to the Saturn sphere, while the Greeks and Romans could reach only up to the sphere of Jupiter. Their consciousness had diminished to a remarkable degree after death. In addition, even their dreamlike picture consciousness had dimmed to the point that only shadowy experiences remained. They thus spoke of the realm of the dead as a dark shadowy place. The ancient Egyptians, on the contrary, still retained lively impressions from this realm, although far less vivid than the ancient Persians or Indians.

The darkening of consciousness was accompanied by an increasing isolation of the human beings after death. It became more and more difficult for them to get in contact with other souls. Rudolf Steiner describes this tragic state for mankind with the following words:

"When the soul left an ancient Indian body and entered the spiritual world, there to pass through the requisite development before the next birth, it retained a living feeling for the spiritual. For, through his whole life the human being of that time yearned for a spiritual environment; and all his sensations were kindled by the revelations he had heard concerning life in the spiritual worlds, even though he was not an initiate himself. So when he passed the portal of death, the spiritual world lay open before him, as it were, in light and radiance.

But in the same measure as the human beings developed sympathy with the physical world and became more skilful in it, the periods between death and rebirth were obscured. In the Egyptian epoch this had gone so far, as can be established by clairvoyant consciousness, that in passing from the body into the spiritual world the soul was enveloped in darkness and gloom. The soul felt lonely and isolated from other souls;[128] *and when a soul feels loneliness and can hold no converse with other souls it experiences a frosty chill.*

And while the Greeks lived in an age in which the humans had made the earth into something quite special by means of such a glorious external beauty in their culture, this period was darkest, gloomiest, most chilling, to the souls living between death and rebirth. And it is not a

---

128 in the later Egyptian period.

legend, but it corresponds to reality that the noble Greek, when asked about the sojourn in the nether world, gave for answer: «Better a beggar in the upper world than a king in the realm of shades».” [129]

With this, mankind was in danger of completely losing the connection with the supersensory worlds. For the dead, these had to become “light and bright” again, so that they could absorb all the necessary forces for their further development and for their next incarnation during their ascent and descent through the spheres. Such a prodigious task of illuminating all these spheres, could be accomplished only by the being who can rightly say of Himself:

“I am the light of the world. He who follows me will not walk in darkness, but shall have the light of life.” (John 8:12)

With the Mystery of Golgotha the conditions in the supersensory worlds changed radically. Rudolf Steiner articulated this in the “Foundation Stone Verse” with the words:

“At the turning point of time the Spirit-light of the world entered the earthly stream of being; darkness of night had ceased its reign; day-bright light shone forth in human souls; light that gives warmth to the poor shepherds' hearts, light that enlightens the wise heads of kings.” [130]

Thus, to all who strive in their minds for an understanding of the Christ event in Palestine 2000 years ago, and who absorb into their hearts the Christ impulse, the path through the individual spheres is

---

129 GA 112 “Das Johannes-Evangelium im Verhältnis zu den drei anderen Evangelien” (The Gospel of John in Relation to the other Three Gospels), Kassel, lecture of June 29, 1909.

130 GA 260 “Die Weihnachtstagung 1923 - 1924” (The Christmas Conference 1923 - 1924), e.g. lecture of December 25, 1923 a.m. - Rudolf Steiner's original words: *“In der Zeiten Wende trat das Welten-Geistes-Licht in den irdischen Wesensstrom; Nacht-Dunkel hatte ausgewaltet; taghelles Licht erstrahlte in Menschenseelen; Licht, das erwärmet die armen Hirtenherzen; Licht, das erleuchtet die weisen Königshäupter.”*

open again, up to the Budhi plane, where the great midnight hour of existence between two incarnations is lived through in union with our true wellspring, with Christ.

He leads us on this path of the great incarnation cycle and therefore speaks of Himself just as rightly: *"I am the way and the truth and the life."* (John 14:6)

And since we have to evolve through the plane of Budhi in order to come to the world of the Father, to the plane of Atma, Christ added to His words the profound truth: *"No one comes to the Father except through me."*

Since the Mystery of Golgotha, it has been possible for people to overcome the "getting younger" of humanity, which was accompanied by a progressive darkening and dulling of consciousness, and instead to climb up again, step by step, the individual stages through which we have all descended. This, however, requires the will of each individual to work on the development of one's own soul and spirit, and the taking in of the Christ impulse.

Hermes Trismegistos, the founder of the Egyptian culture, once proclaimed the great law of correspondences: as in the large, so in the small; as above, so below; as outside, so inside. According to this cosmic law all supersensory planes of existence, which we wander through, are mirrored in the seven-year periods of our earthly lives. Figure 18 shows the experiences associated with the individual spheres and ages.

In the meantime we have descended to the materialistic world view, because without our contribution we mature at most up to the age of 27. As a result, we are only receptive to the influence from the Mars sphere, which alone contains the spiritual archetypes of the lifeless things in the physical world. The understanding for life as a supersensory power, which the Greeks still had, has been lost to the vast majority of humanity.

		planes of existence	ages		cultures	experiences	seven-year periods
Budhi	1	1st sphere of the Budhi plane	♎	Atlantean	primeval Semites	the Spirit of Life	11th seven-year period (age 70 – 77)
Spiritual World	7	sphere of the germ sheath of the spirit man	♍		Akkadians	divine order and laws	10th seven-year period (age 63 – 70)
	6	sphere of the germ sheath of the life spirit	♌		Mongols	life force	9th seven-year period (age 56 – 63)
	5	sphere of the spirit self	♋	post–Atlantean	primeval Indians	Review of previous incarnations	8th seven-year period (age 49 – 56)
	4	sphere of the zodiac	♊		primeval Persians	Zodiacus und Sun Spirit	7th seven-year period (age 42 – 49)
	3	Saturn sphere	♉		Egyptians/ Chaldeans/ Babylonians	soul of the World	6th seven-year period (age 35 – 42)
	2	Jupiter sphere	♈		Greeks/ Romans	life rhythm in nature	5th seven-year period (age 28 – 35)
	1	Mars sphere	♓		Germanic peoples/ Anglo-Saxons	materialism	4th seven-year period (age 21 – 28)

Figure 18: Development of the human consciousness in the different ages and in the seven-year periods of earthly life

However, if we continue to strive to mature in soul and spirit as we ascend from one seven-year period to the next, we will grow in consciousness towards the Budhi plane and thus towards Christ. From the age of 70 we become particularly receptive to His influences raying down from the first sphere of the Budhi plane.

On a small scale, our path through the seven-year periods of life on earth runs analogous to the great path of our incarnation cycle, on which Christ also guides us up to His world, the world of the life spirit.

Thus, only by connecting with Christ during the earthly life will the light shine brightly again for us in the world beyond.

"Only through Christ having come to earth, and through the human beings having received knowledge of a Christ in a preparatory way in the time of the Old Testament; only because the human beings had integrated the figure of the Christ into the mind, into the imagination here in earthly life, could they take along from the physical world to the hereafter that which brought light again to them in the world beyond. What they took along made the other side clear and bright again and restored the Christ to them with even greater splendour than in this world. Hence, we see how consciousness on the other side became darkened more and more as the time approached which we described yesterday; and how it then brightens up by the fact that man in this world gets to know the Christ, that he learns what is reported of the Christ. For what man learns of Him in this world is not lost in the period between death and rebirth; he takes his knowledge with him; and this is what the expression "To die into Christ" means." [131]

Thus, if by grace we are granted the 11th seven-year period on earth, from the age of 70 to 77, the period into which primarily the

[131] GA 105 "Welt, Erde und Mensch" (World, Earth and the Human Being), Stuttgart, lecture of August 14, 1908.

first sphere of the Budhi plane is mirrored which is related to the physical body and the outer earthly world (as it is the case with all first spheres of the different worlds), it behoves us to make our own to the greatest degree the descriptions of the earthly life of Christ in the physical body, so that the historic Christ can become Christ in us. Should this be the case, then at the end of the earthly life, unlike in pre-Christian times we may enter the worlds beyond with awake I-consciousness.

"Humanity could never carry the I-consciousness beyond death unless this I-consciousness, having developed in the physical body, unites with the Christ who holds and supports it when it would otherwise melt away from the human soul along with the physical body. The I-consciousness is acquired by means of the physical body. In death it would melt away with the physical body from the human soul, if the «I» were not bound up with the Christ Being in the sense of St. Paul's words, «Not I but Christ in me» — for the Christ takes the I and carries it through death."[132]

The 12th Seven-Year Period and the Second Sphere of the Budhi plane (Age: 77 – 84 Years)

Through the Mystery of Golgotha, Christ has reopened to us the entire path from the earth up to the Budhi plane, which had become increasingly closed to humanity in the pre-Christian ages. In this way he has created the necessary conditions, so that during the great midnight hour of existence between two incarnations, we can receive

132 GA 215 "Die Philosophie, Kosmologie und Religion in der Anthroposophie" (Philosophy, Cosmology and Religion in Anthroposophy), Dornach, lecture of September 13, 1922.

those powers from the Budhi plane which we need so that the Budhi can enter into us during life on earth. Rudolf Steiner drew our attention to this most significant fact:

"Through the deed of Christ on earth, the rudiments were formed in the human beings that they could receive what we call Budhi into their Manas. [...]

What entered into the physical, etheric, and astral body of Jesus of Nazareth was the entirety of this Fire Spirit, the common source of all spirit sparks bestowed on humanity. This is the Christ, the only divine being, which, in this way, does not exist in any other form on earth. He entered the Jesus of Nazareth, in order that those who felt connected with the Christ Jesus received the power to absorb the Budhi into themselves. The possibility of receiving the Budhi begins with the appearance of Christ Jesus. This is what John called the divine Creator-Word. The divine Creator-Word is this Fire Spirit who poured out his sparks into the human beings." [133]

Like every world, the Budhi plane is composed of seven regions or spheres. The first or lowest sphere of the Budhi plane is related to the human physical body. The revelation of Christ to humanity began when He himself came before them in his physical form. This transpired from the baptism at the Jordan River, when Christ descended into the physical body of Jesus of Nazareth, and, thus, for the first time, connected the Budhi with a physical human form. Thereby, the door to the first region of the Budhi plane had been opened to mankind.

Ever since, all those who during earthly life connect inwardly with Christ can receive after their death, at the great midnight hour of

---

133 GA 97 "Das christliche Mysterium" (The Christian Mystery), Cologne, lecture of December 2, 1906.

existence in the middle between two incarnations, the power of the life spirit from the first sphere of the Budhi plane. Therefore, even before the Mystery of Golgotha, Christ could initiate John the Baptist in his spiritual development up to the Budhi plane.

"John had to develop himself up to the Budhi to become able to understand what was manifesting in the Christ Jesus." [134]

Before the Mystery of Golgotha, however, this high level of initiation could only be accomplished if the person to be initiated laid aside his physical body beforehand. He had to pass through the gate of death. For this, it had to be allowed that John the Baptist was murdered.

Afterwards, Lazarus also was permitted to partake in the initiation reaching up to the Budhi plane. In the course of his "awakening" or "raising" he was surrounded by the spiritual members of the deceased John the Baptist, who had been initiated up to the Budhi plane. The resulting double entity of Lazarus-John was the Christ's "favourite disciple" and the first human being "fashioned" after Him, i.e., reaching from earth up to the Budhi plane. Lazarus alone could not have reached up to the Budhi and the deceased John the Baptist could not have reached down to the physical body.

This condition concerning the initiation up to the Budhi changed for humanity only after Christ himself had carried life through the gate of death in the course of the Mystery of Golgotha. His resurrection body, in which he appeared to those closest to him, was a kind of transitional state between the physical body and the etheric life body. Only on account of Christ's mediation could He become visible to his disciples. His appearance, however, was not identical to the physical

---

134 GA 94 "Kosmogonie" (Cosmogony), Munich, October 28, 1906.

body placed in the tomb. Therefore, as reported in the gospels, the disciples could not at first recognize Him as the Risen One.[135]

With the Ascension, the risen Christ moved into the etheric sphere or the earth's life body and became invisible even to the disciples. However, with his deed, he opened for them the access to the second sphere of the Budhi plane, which relates to the life or etheric body. Thereby, the Christ created conditions by which he can appear to human beings in his etheric body in the future, and elevate them one level higher. The entire ether region of the earth was to be made accessible again to humanity during life on earth.

To this effect, the powers of the intellect and the human I had to be sufficiently strengthened. This was precisely the purpose served by the Kali Yuga or the Dark Age, during which mankind was temporarily deprived of the direct view into the higher worlds and, for a given period, the consciousness was directed entirely on the physical world. Towards the end of the Kali Yuga in 1899, the forces of the intellect and their bearer, the etheric body, as well as the I-consciousness had developed to such a degree that a new period of time could begin in which people will develop a new clairvoyance. Since the 20th century it is therefore possible that Christ appears in the etheric body.

"In the fourth post-Atlantean cultural epoch the Christ Being who descended from cosmic heights had first to appear in a physical body. In our fifth cultural epoch the intellectual forces will intensify in such a way that the human being will be enabled to behold the Christ not as a physical but as an etheric figure. This is even now beginning in our century. From the thirties to the forties of this century onwards, individuals will appear who have developed their individuality in a way that will enable them to see the etheric form of Christ, as at the time of

---

135 Mark 16:12 f., Luke 24:13 f. and John 20:19 f.

Jesus of Nazareth they saw the physical Christ. And during the next three thousand years the number of those able to behold the etheric Christ will steadily increase, until in about three thousand years, reckoning from the present time, there will be a sufficient number of human beings on the Earth who will need no gospels or other such records, because in the soul they will have seen the Christ."[136]

"In the soul", that is, not with physical eyes, but by means of the new clairvoyance they will see the Christ. However, in order to understand what they will then see and to recognize its importance, sufficient preparation through the teachings of spiritual science is required.

"Those persons who will let themselves be stimulated by spiritual science will, from the middle of the twentieth century onward, gradually become able to experience a renewal of what St. Paul saw in etheric clairvoyance as mystery to come, the Mystery of the Living Christ."[137]

The apostle Paul was enabled to see the living Christ as an etheric figure ahead of time, because Christ Himself intervened directly and "opened his sight". In a similar way, He had made it possible for the disciples to see His resurrection body. Neither could transpire without His direct intervention. Paul knew that his vision was an exception, an untimely experience. That is why he said of himself, *"Then, last of all, He was seen also by me, as by one born out of due time."* (1 Corinthians 15:8)

In the course of the third millennium, at the beginning of which we are standing, this vision will become possible for more and more

---

136 GA 130 "Das esoterische Christentum und die geistige Führung der Menschheit" (Esoteric Christianity and the Spiritual Guidance of Mankind), Milano (Italy), lecture of September 21, 1911.

137 GA 121 "Die Mission einzelner Volksseelen" (The Mission of Individual Folk Souls", Kristiania (Oslo, Norway), lecture of June 17, 1910.

people. Already since the 20th century we can be guided during life after death by Christ up to the domain of the Budhi plane, in order to be filled, at the great midnight hour of existence, with forces of its second sphere, the sphere which is specifically connected with the etheric body.

For this reason, meditations on the weekly verses of Rudolf Steiner's Anthroposophical Soul Calendar, guide the meditant's feeling through the individual spheres up to the second sphere of the Budhi plane. If we enhance our sensitivity by means of these weekly verses, we prepare ourselves to sustain our consciousness longer during the next after-death ascent into the higher worlds, and to better understand the experiences which we may encounter there. In this way, we will enable us to avail ourselves of a greater amount of the forces offered to us and carry them down into the next earthly life. The author has described these connections in detail in his book "The Anthroposophical Soul Calendar and the Incarnation Cycle of Man".

The more consciously we have lived through the individual stages of our existence in the higher worlds, the more clearly they will be mirrored in the seven-year periods of our subsequent life on earth. At the age of 77 to 84 years, should such grace befall us, we may become especially receptive to an after-effect of the highest event that can be reached by us between two incarnations, namely, the contact with the second sphere of the Budhi plane at the great midnight hour of existence.

The years of the 12th seven-year period are therefore particularly suitable for turning to the phenomenon of Christ's return in the etheric form. Whoever devotes himself intimately to this subject will thereby prepare himself for the encounter with Him, regardless of whether it will take place already before death or only afterwards.

We have seen that with each seven-year period which we are allowed to experience on earth, we actually come closer and closer to Christ, grow and mature towards Him.

The 13th and 14th Seven-Year Periods (Age: 84 – 91 Years und 91 – 98 Years)

The inflow of the Budhi into humanity takes place in several steps. Should this transpire in a comprehensive way, as is necessary for mankind to reach its goal of development by the end of the earth's existence, forces from even further regions of the Budhi plane must likewise become accessible. Through this, Christ will be able to reveal Himself to us in ever exalted way.

"The next event, then, is that human beings will see Christ on the astral plane in etheric form, and those who are then living on the physical plane, and who have absorbed the teachings of Spiritual Science, will perceive Him. Those, however, who are then no longer living, but who have prepared themselves through spiritual-scientific work will see Him, nonetheless, in etheric raiment between their death and rebirth. [...]

Then will come an era when still higher powers will awaken in human beings. This will be the era when the Christ will manifest Himself in a still loftier manner; in an astral form in the lower world of Devachan.

And in the final era of moral impulses the human beings who have passed through the former stages will behold the Christ in His glory, as the form of the greatest "I", as the spiritualised I-Self, as the great Teacher of human evolution in the higher Devachan."[138]

The age in which Christ will appear in an astral form in the lower spiritual world is the age of Aquarius, which will follow our age. With an average duration of the ages of 2,160 years, it will extend from the year 3573 to the year 5733 A.D.

The following age, in which Christ will show himself *"as the form of the greatest I"* in the higher spiritual world, is the age of Capricorn. It is the seventh and last age of the first great post-Atlantean epoch, which will begin with the year 5733 and end with the "war of all against all".

In the chapter on the 11th seven-year period it has already been explained that at the age of 70 to 77 we become particularly receptive to influences from the first sphere of the Budhi plane, which is connected with the physical body as well as with the appearance of Christ in physical form on earth.

In the chapter on the 12th seven-year period, at the age of 77 to 84, our receptivity to the influences from the second sphere of the Budhi plane was described. These are related to the ether body and make it possible to behold the appearance of Christ in etheric form.

Therefore, when considering the 13th seven-year period, the question arises whether at the age of 84 to 91, we are already becoming receptive to influences from the third sphere of the Budhi plane, which is connected with the astral body and will make possible the appearance of Christ in astral form? And at the still later age of 91 to 98 years, can we possibly even already become receptive to forces from the fourth sphere of the Budhi plane, which will have an

---

138 GA 130 "Das esoterische Christentum und die geistige Führung der Menschheit" (Esoteric Christianity and the Spiritual Guidance of Mankind) Leipzig, lecture of November 4, 1911.

influence on the human I and make possible the revelation of the Christ as macrocosmic I?

These two questions must certainly be answered in the negative, for such receptivity would require that Christ has already opened for us access to the third and fourth spheres of the Budhi plane today, so that in the middle between two incarnations, in the great midnight hour of existence, we could receive forces from there. This, however, is not the case, but it will rather occur in the next era and the one that follows. Until then, it behoves to us to deepen our relationship to the etheric Christ, which can be best accomplished through a deeper study of Anthroposophy.

Something else remains to be considered. In order for humans to come into contact with the forces of the t h i r d sphere of the Budhi plane, they must be lifted out of the lowest sphere of the physical world and from the physical human bodies belonging to it. Already at our present stage of development, in which the powers of the s e c o n d sphere of the Budhi plane have opened for us the possibility of meeting Christ in his etheric form, we are no longer as closely connected with our physical bodies as was the case for the ancient Greeks.

"Actually, with each incarnation we withdraw more and more from the corporeality and are rather hovering above the corporeality. If this were not the case, the further development of mankind would be in a bad way. If the human being was to depend entirely on being like the ancient Greeks, the prospects for the further development of mankind would be dire indeed."[139]

---

[139] GA 177 "Die spirituellen Hintergründe der physischen Welt – Der Sturz der Geister der Finsternis" (The Spiritual Background of the Physical World – The Fall of the Spirits of Darkness), Dornach, lecture of October 7, 1917.

Each opening of another sphere of the Budhi plane makes it more difficult to incarnate in a physical body. This will lead to a momentous change for humanity. At the beginning of the Aquarian age, in the year 3573, human beings will still mature up to the age of 21 due to the general "getting younger". However, at the end of the Aquarian age, that is at the beginning of the age of Capricorn, in 5733, they will only be able to mature up to the age of 14! This is the age at which the reproductive organs complete their physical maturation. The further "getting younger" of mankind is therefore connected with an increasing loss of the physical body's possibility of reproduction.

"A year will come in the physical evolution of the earth — it will be, let us say, about the year 5700 or a bit more – in this year, or around this year, the human beings will no longer tread the earth by incarnating in bodies derived from physical parents, if the human evolution takes place in a rightful way over the whole earth. In that epoch, women will be barren, as I often said; children will no longer be born in the manner of today, if evolution all over the earth takes its normal course."[140]

However, it is to be expected that the normal evolution up to 5700, that is until the late 6th millennium A.D., will be exposed to a powerful Ahrimanic influence with the aim to prolong the possibility to incarnate in physical bodies beyond the normal evolution, up to the 7th millennium, though in a wrongful way.

"There must be no misunderstanding about such a fact as this. Something else, for example, might come about. The Ahrimanic Powers, which under the influence of the impulses working in men to-day are becoming extremely strong, might divert the earth-evolution; they could

140 GA 196 "Geistige und soziale Wandlungen in der Menschheitsentwicklung" (Spiritual and Social Transformations in human Evolution), Dornach, lecture of January 18, 1920.

pervert the earth evolution in a certain sense. Then, it would become possible for the human beings — by no means for their good — to be held in the same form of physical life beyond this time in the sixth millennium. But they would become much more like animals, while continuing to be held in the grip of physical incarnation. One of the endeavours of the Ahrimanic Powers is to keep humanity fettered too long to the earth in order to divert it from its normal evolution.

However, if mankind really takes hold of the best possibilities of its evolution, then in the sixth millennium it will enter for further 2,500 years into a connection with the earthly world of such a kind that the human beings will still have a relationship with the earth, but a relationship no longer coming to expression in the birth of physical children. In order to make the picture graphic, I will put it like this: the human beings will be astir in clouds, in rain, in lightning and thunder, as beings of spirit-and-soul in the affairs of the earth. They will pulse, as it were, through the phenomena of nature; and in a still later epoch their relationship to the earthly will become even more spiritual."[141]

In another lecture Rudolf Steiner said on the same subject:

"Things will, however, become somewhat more difficult when in the future, approximately in the 6th or 7th millennium of the earth's evolution, man will take on a completely different form. You will be surprised that I say this. But it is actually the case, because in the 6th or 7th millennium women will become infertile, will no longer come to maturity, but will remain infertile. The human being will then be in connection with the earth in a much more spiritual form."[142]

---

141 Ibidem.

142 GA 343a "2. Priesterkurs" (2nd priest course), Dornach, lecture of October 6, 1921, in the afternoon.

During the course of the age of Capricorn, in which people will be able to mature according to the general "getting younger" only up to the 14th year of life, and, finally, only up to the 7th year of life, the possibility of incarnation in a physical human body will be lost.

The two following ages of Sagittarius and Scorpio, which are related to the 1st seven-year period and the embryonic life in the process of the "getting younger" of mankind, belong to the sixth great epoch or second great post-Atlantean epoch, after the Great War of all against all. Then a completely new order will prevail on earth with an etheric humanity which will only loosely connect with physical substances. In this, the second great earth epoch will find its mirroring, the Hyperborean epoch, when people enveloped themselves only with etheric bodies and hovered in the atmosphere above the glowing earth.

The incarnation of human beings began only during the third great epoch of earth's evolution, the Lemurian epoch. The incarnations will naturally cease at the end of the fifth great epoch. We therefore remain "earth beings" only for a limited span of time. Truly, we are cosmic beings.

In the sixth great epoch, one will no longer be able to speak of an "incarnation cycle", because then we will no longer descend so far as the flesh, i.e., incarnate ("carne", Latin for flesh). In its place, the great "life cycle" will lead us to ever higher spheres of the Budhi plane. With the help of the forces streaming to us from there, we will, at the end of the earth evolution, entirely detach ourselves from the physical globe and, with Christ's guidance, pass into an astral condition and continue our evolution on higher levels.

List of Figures

ROLAND SCHRAPP
The Anthroposophical
Soul Calendar and
the Incarnation Cycle of Man
The Spiritual Archetype underlying the Soul Calendar

Roland Schrapp

Publisher:
BoD – Books on Demand,
Norderstedt (Germany)

Large format (DIN A4)
270 pages, 27 illustrations

Paperback (adhesive binding):
ISBN-13: 978-3752690101
ISBN-10: 3752690100

Hardcover (thread binding):
ISBN-13: 978-3752602906
ISBN-10: 3752602902

This book takes a completely new look at the Anthroposophical Soul Calendar. It is about the deeper meaning of the fifty-two weekly verses, which has remained essentially unexplored in the last hundred years since the first edition by Rudolf Steiner. A dense veil of Isis was spread over them, of which is well known that no mortal person can lift it. Only the immortal, psycho-spiritual human being, who knows himself at home in the extrasensory, higher worlds, is capable of doing this. Only to him the weekly verses reveal themselves as a travel guide through these worlds and lift him up to ever higher spiritual-cosmic realms until he reaches the experience of God, from where he gradually descends again into a new life on Earth, enriched in spirit and fertilized in his soul. If the reader embarks on this journey, the spiritual archetype of the Soul Calendar is ultimately unveiled to him and he achieves an extended understanding of Man and Christ. By many quotations from Rudolf Steiner's lectures and books, the author virtually lets Steiner himself elucidate the breathtaking depths of his mysterious weekly verses.

Roland Schrapp

Publisher:
BoD – Books on Demand

Paperback:
81 pages, 6 illustrations

ISBN-13: 978-3754396261
ISBN-10: 3754396269

This book is not a mere summary of Rudolf Steiner's statements on the connection of the forces of the zodiac with the ages, but it offers a whole new range of view points on astrology, astronomy and the cultural history of mankind. The author first describes the origin of the zodiacal images according to Rudolf Steiner's statements. Then he discusses why these images do not correspond either with the signs of the zodiac in traditional astrology or with the physically visible constellations of the stars, and what role the astronomy of the ancient Greeks plays in this. It is also explained why, when creating a horoscope, the planetary positions must not simply be taken over unchanged from the ephemerides. They need a correction due to the precession of the vernal equinox. This makes the book a "must have" for every astrologically interested person. Another topic is the varying duration of the ages and what questions this raises for modern astronomy. Finally, using the example of European cultural development over the last thousand years, it is shown that each age is divided into twelve smaller cultural periods, which in their characteristics correspond exactly to the series of the zodiacal forces. In this way it becomes understandable why the cultural development of mankind just happened the way it did.

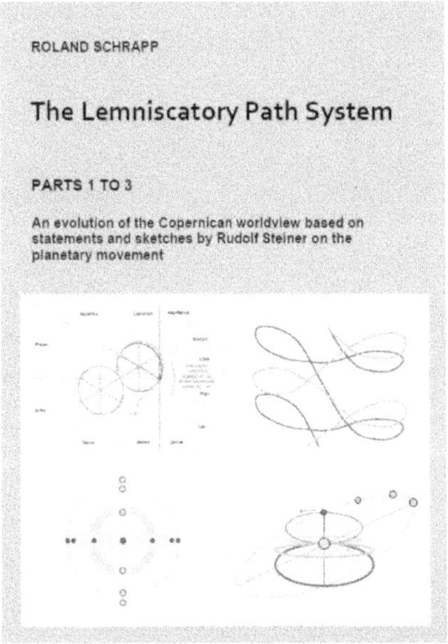
ROLAND SCHRAPP
The Lemniscatory Path System
PARTS 1 TO 3
An evolution of the Copernican worldview based on statements and sketches by Rudolf Steiner on the planetary movement

Roland Schrapp

Publisher:
BoD – Books on Demand,
Norderstedt (Germany)

Paperback: 198 pages
Large format (DIN A4)
253 mostly coloured illustrations

ISBN-13: 978-3752604030
ISBN-10: 3752604034

An evolution of the Copernican worldview based on statements and sketches by Rudolf Steiner on the planetary movement.

For the first time in almost a hundred years, Rudolf Steiner's statements and sketches on the subject of the "lemniscatory paths of the planets", distributed over several lecture cycles, have been brought into a larger context and examined for the consequences of this. Steiner's suggestions for a new consideration of the planetary movement were taken up and tried to develop them further in the given sense. The work "The Lemniscatory Path System" arose from this. The treatise comprises 192 pages with 253 mostly coloured illustrations.

Ingram Content Group UK Ltd.
Milton Keynes UK
UKHW011820160323
418676UK00001B/107

9 783743 124585